GCSE Edexcel 360Science
Biology
The Workbook

This book is for anyone doing **GCSE Edexcel 360Science Biology**.

It's full of **tricky questions**... each one designed to make you **sweat** — because that's the only way you'll get any **better**.

There are questions to see **what facts** you know. There are questions to see how well you can **apply those facts**. And there are questions to see what you know about **how science works**.

It's also got some daft bits in to try and make the whole experience at least vaguely entertaining for you.

What CGP is all about

Our sole aim here at CGP is to produce the highest quality books — carefully written, immaculately presented and dangerously close to being funny.

Then we work our socks off to get them out to you — at the cheapest possible prices.

Contents

B1a Topic 1 — Environment

Energy and Biomass 1
Competition and Populations 2
Evolution .... Audio Part 1 + 2 ✓ 4
Natural Selection 5
Classification 7
Changing Species' Characteristics 8
Human Activity and the Environment ..... Audio 1 + 2 ✓ 9

B1a Topic 2 — Genes

Variation in Plants and Animals 13
DNA and Genes 15
Asexual Reproduction 16
Sexual Reproduction and Variation .... Audio 1 + 2 17
Genetic Diagrams 19
The Human Genome Project 21
Genetic Engineering 22
Genetic Disorders and Gene Therapy 23
Cloning 24
Mixed Questions — B1a Topics 1 & 2 26

B1b Topic 3 — Electrical & Chemical Signals

The Nervous System 28
The Central Nervous System 30
Voluntary and Reflex Responses 32
Examples of Reflex Actions 34
The Blood 35
Hormones 36
Hormones — Insulin and Diabetes 37
Hormones — The Menstrual Cycle 39
Hormones — Fertility 41

B1b Topic 4 — Use, Misuse and Abuse

The Body's Defence Systems 42
Infectious Diseases 43
TB — Tuberculosis 45
Drugs 47
Drugs — Use and Harm 48
Painkillers 50
Mixed Questions — B1b Topics 3 & 4 52

B2 Topic 1 — Inside Living Cells

Respiration 54
Respiration and Exercise 55
Evaluating Health Claims 57
DNA — Making Proteins 59
Using Microorganisms 60

B2 Topic 2 — Divide and Develop

Growth in Organisms 63
Cell Division — Mitosis 64
Cell Division — Meiosis 65
Stem Cells and Differentiation 66
Growth in Plants 67
Growth in Plants: Plant Hormones 68
Selective Breeding 69
Cloning and Genetic Modification 71
Gene Therapy 73
Mixed Questions — B2 Topics 1 & 2 74

B2 Topic 3 — Energy Flow

Plants and Photosynthesis 78
Rate of Photosynthesis 79
The Carbon Cycle 81
Minerals and Plants 83
The Nitrogen Cycle 84
Life on Mars 85
There's Too Many People 87
Climate Change and Food Distribution 89
Food Production 90

B2 Topic 4 — Interdependence

Population Sizes 91
Extreme Environments 93
Air Pollution — CO_2 and CO 95
Interpreting Data: Climate Change 96
Air Pollution — Acid Rain 97
Water Pollution 98
Living Indicators 100
Conservation 102
Recycling 103
Mixed Questions — B2 Topics 3 & 4 105

B3 Topic 1 — Biotechnology

Microorganisms and Food 108
Diet and Obesity 111
Genetically Modifying Plants 112
New Treatments — Drugs 115
New Treatments — Using Genetics 116
Reproductive Technology 117
Stem Cells 119
Mixed Questions — B3 Topic 1 121

B3 Topic 2 — Behaviour in Humans and Other Animals

Instinctive and Learned Behaviour 123
Social Behaviour and Communication 126
Feeding Behaviours 128
Reproductive Behaviours 131
Human Evolution and Development 135
Human Behaviour Towards Animals 137
Mixed Questions — B3 Topic 2 138

Published by Coordination Group Publications Ltd.

Editors:
Amy Boutal, Ellen Bowness, Tom Cain, Sarah Hilton, Kate Houghton, Rose Parkin,
Kate Redmond, Laurence Stamford.

Contributors:
Bridie Begbie, Claire Charlton, Jane Davies, Catherine Debley, Sarah Evans, James Foster,
Dr Iona M J Hamilton, Derek Harvey, Rebecca Harvey, Andy Rankin, Adrian Schmit,
Claire Stebbing, Sidney Stringer Community School, Paul Warren, Anna-Fe Williamson,
Dee Wyatt.

ISBN: 978 1 84146 668 2

With thanks to Sue Hocking and Glenn Rogers for the proofreading.
With thanks to Jan Greenway and Katie Steele for the copyright research.

Graph of sulphur dioxide emissions on page 9 compiled by NETCEN on behalf of the Department of the Environment, Food and Rural Affairs.

Graph of ozone concentration on page 9 and graph on page 11 produced with permission of Earth System Research Laboratory, National Oceanic and Atmospheric Administration.

Map of sulphur dioxide pollution on page 11 based on data produced and copyrighted by the Centre for Ecology and Hydrology.

Graph on page 30 reproduced with kind permission from the British Heart Foundation © 2006.

Source of graph on page 45: The United Kingdom Parliament. Parliamentary material is reproduced with the permission of the Controller of HMSO on behalf of Parliament.

Graph of percentage of waste recycled in England on page 88 from the e-digest environmental statistics website: http://www.defra.gov.uk/environment/statistics. Crown Copyright material is reproduced with the permission of the Controller of HMSO.

Graph of cod and herring stocks on page 92 from www.statistics.gov.uk. Crown Copyright material is reproduced with the permission of the Controller of HMSO.

Graph of global temperature variation 1700-2000 on page 96 reproduced with permission of the Climatic Research Unit, School of Environmental Sciences, University of East Anglia: www.cru@uea.ac.uk.

Data to construct graph on page 104 is from Defra and is reproduced under the terms of the Click-Use Licence.

Groovy website: www.cgpbooks.co.uk

Printed by Elanders Hindson Ltd, Newcastle upon Tyne.
Jolly bits of clipart from CorelDRAW®

Text, design, layout and original illustrations © Coordination Group Publications Ltd. 2006
All rights reserved.

B1a Topic 1 — Environment

Energy and Biomass

Q1 A single **robin** has a mass of 15 g and eats caterpillars. Each robin eats 25 **caterpillars** that each have a mass of 2 g. The caterpillars feed on 10 **stinging nettles** that together have a mass of 500 g. Study the pyramid diagrams shown and then answer the questions that follow.

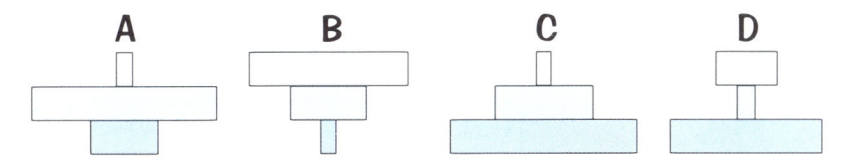

A   B   C   D

a) Which diagram is most likely to represent a pyramid of **numbers** for these organisms? ....

b) Which is most likely to represent a pyramid of **biomass** for these organisms? ....

c) Explain how you decided on your answer to part **b)** above.

....

d) The stinging nettles are the first trophic level. Where does their energy initially come from?

....

Q2 Read the sentences below about **food chains** and **energy transfer**. Then tick the boxes to show which sentences are true and which are false.

		True	False
a)	The Sun is the source of the energy used by nearly all life on Earth.	☐	☐
b)	Plants convert all the light energy that falls on them into glucose.	☐	☐
c)	Energy is used in respiration at each stage in a food chain.	☐	☐
d)	For a given area of land it is usually more efficient to grow crops for food than to graze animals for the meat.	☐	☐
e)	Only energy is passed between the steps of food chains.	☐	☐
f)	Animals that have to maintain a constant body temperature lose more energy as heat than animals that don't.	☐	☐

Q3 Complete the sentences below by **circling** the most appropriate word each time.

a) Life on Earth depends on **food** / **energy** from the Sun.

b) **Plants** / **Animals** can make their own food by a process called **photosynthesis** / **respiration**.

c) To obtain energy animals must **decay** / **eat** plant material or other animals.

d) Animals release energy from food through the process of **photosynthesis** / **respiration**.

e) Some of the energy obtained by animals from their food is **gained** / **lost** before it reaches organisms at later steps of the food chain. This is mainly because it has been used for **growth** / **movement**.

Competition and Populations

Q1 Indicate whether each behaviour involves animals trying to **compete** (**C**) or acting as **predators** (**P**) by putting a tick in the correct column.

BEHAVIOUR	C	P
Stags grow antlers during the mating season		
A pack of wolves work together to kill a moose		
A magpie chases a sparrow away from a bird-table		
Spiders spin webs to trap flies		
Lions chase leopards and cheetahs from their territory		

Q2 **Algae** are tiny photosynthetic organisms that are eaten by **fish**. The graph shows how the size of a population of algae in a pond varied throughout one year.

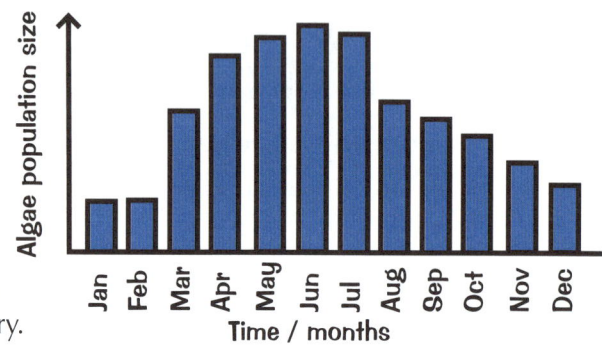

a) Suggest **two conditions** that may have changed in the pond to give more algae in June than in January.

....

b) The number of **fish** in the pond increased rapidly during **one month** of the year. Suggest which month this was. Explain your answer.

....

....

Q3 Jenny cultured some **bacterial cells** in a liquid medium. She counted the number of cells at intervals as they multiplied. Her results are shown in the table.

Time / minutes	No. of bacterial cells
0	1
20	2
40	4
60	8
80	16
100	32
120	64

a) Suggest **two** things Jenny had to provide the bacteria with to allow them to grow.

1. ....

2. ....

b) Calculate the number of bacteria you would expect to find after **3 hours**.

Hint: look for a pattern in Jenny's results and then just continue it.

....

c) After 3 hours, Jenny found that the number of bacteria had in fact begun to **decrease**. Suggest why this might be.

....

....

d) What type of **competition** is occurring in the medium? ....

B1a Topic 1 — Environment

Competition and Populations

Q4 The graph below shows how the sizes of a population of **deer** and a population of **wolves** living in the same area changed over time.

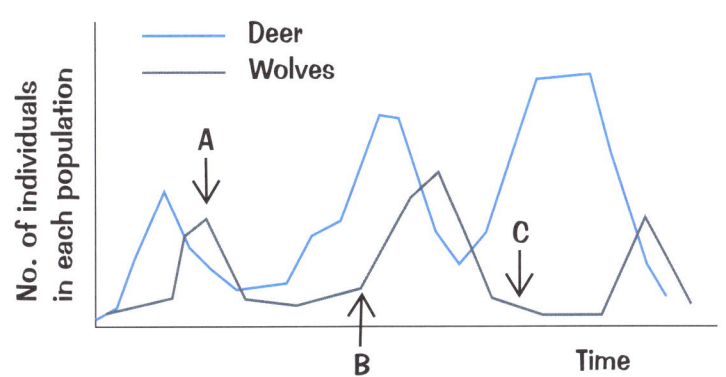

a) Describe the pattern in the changing sizes of these two populations.

....

....

....

b) i) Explain **why** the two populations are connected in this way.

....

ii) What is this **relationship** called? ....

c) At one point during the period covered by this graph, the wolves were affected by a **disease**. Underline one of the options below to show when this was.

        At point A   At point B   At point C

d) What effect did the disease have on the size of the **deer** population? Why was this?

....

....

Q5 In Britain, the population of **red squirrels** is declining and may eventually disappear completely. Scientists used a **computer model** to study this problem.

a) State **two advantages** of using a computer model rather than counting squirrels in the wild.

1. ....

2. ....

b) State **two disadvantages** of using computer modelling.

1. ....

2. ....

B1a Topic 1 — Environment

Evolution

Q1 Dinosaurs, mammoths and dodos are all animals that are now **extinct**.

a) What does the term 'extinct' mean?

....

....

b) What **evidence** is there to show that extinct animals ever existed?

....

....

Q2 Fossils were found in this sample of **rock**.

a) Explain why scientists think that fossil B is **older**.

....

....

....

b) Give **two** ways in which fossils can be **formed**.

1. ....

2. ....

Q3 **A** and **B** are **fossilised bones** from the legs of ancestors of the modern **horse**. Some scientists believe that animals with legs like those in fossil A gradually developed into animals with legs like those in fossil B.

a) Explain what advantages animals with legs like those in fossil B would have had over those with legs like those in fossil A.

....

....

....

b) It is thought that there was a stage in the development of the horse between A and B, during which the leg bone would have looked like C. Suggest why **no fossils** of C have been found.

....

....

Top Tip: Fossils tend to conjure up images of creaky old scientists, or worse, Ross Geller armed with his fossil brush. But they're the only way we have of knowing about crazy creatures like T. Rex, mammoths, ancient horses the size of dogs and rodents that stood two metres high (seriously).

B1a Topic 1 — Environment

Natural Selection

Q1 Explain what Darwin meant when he said that natural selection happens by 'survival of the fittest'.

....

....

....

Q2 Which of the statements below gives a reason why some scientists did **not** at first agree with Darwin's ideas about **natural selection**? Circle the letter next to the correct statement.

   A   He could not explain how characteristics could be inherited.

   B   Characteristics that are caused by the environment can be inherited.

   C   They thought he was making up the evidence.

   D   They felt that Darwin was influenced by religious rather than scientific ideas.

Q3 Giraffes used to have much **shorter** necks than they do today.
The statements below explain Darwin's theory about how their neck length changed.
Write numbers in the boxes to show the **order** the statements should be in.

   [2] The giraffes competed for food from low branches. This food started to become scarce. Many giraffes died before they could breed.

   [5] More long-necked giraffes survived to breed, so more giraffes were born with long necks.

   [ ] A giraffe was born with a longer neck than normal. The long-necked giraffe was able to eat more food.

   [1] All giraffes had short necks.

   [4] The long-necked giraffe survived to have lots of offspring that all had longer necks.

   [6] All giraffes had long necks.

Q4 Peahens select mates based on the **size** and **colour** of their tails. But males with large, brightly coloured tails have a **decreased** chance of survival. Explain why a gene that gives males a larger tail but decreases their chances of survival would probably become **common** in a population.

....

....

....

B1a Topic 1 — Environment

Natural Selection

Q5 Millions of years ago, North and South America were **separate land masses**. Due to movements of the Earth's crust, they then **joined together**. The mammals in North America were '**placental**' (they gave birth to well-developed babies) and those in South America were '**marsupial**' (they gave birth to under-developed babies which developed in a 'pouch' of their mother's skin).

After North and South America joined, nearly all the marsupials became **extinct**. Suggest two reasons why this may have happened.

....

....

....

....

....

Q6 The **peppered moth** is an insect that is often found on tree bark and is preyed on by birds. There are **two varieties** of peppered moth — a light form and a dark form. Until the 1850s, the **light form** was more common, but then the **dark form** became more widespread, particularly near cities.

Moths on tree bark in unpolluted area

Moths on tree bark in polluted area

a) Why do you think the lighter variety of the peppered moth was more common originally?

....

....

Hint: Use the diagrams to help you.

b) In the 1850s, the Industrial Revolution began — there was rapid growth in heavy industries in Britain. Why do you think the number of dark moths increased after this time?

....

....

c) Do you think a difference in genes or in environment would cause a dark moth to suddenly appear in a population of light moths? ....

B1a Topic 1 — Environment

Classification

Q1 Which of the following is the **best** definition of a **species**? Tick one box.

☐ A group of organisms that look very similar to one another.

☑ A group of closely-related organisms that can interbreed successfully.

☐ A classification group containing only a few different types of organism.

Q2 Gnus are large **mammals** that roam the Serengeti.
They have the scientific name ***Connochaetes gnou***.

a) Complete the table below to show how gnus are classified.

Kingdom	....	....	....	....	Genus	....
Animalia	Chordata	Mammalia	Artiodactyla	Bovidae		....

b) Give two features all mammals have in common that can be useful when classifying them.

1. ....

2. ....

Q3 Animals can be classified as **vertebrates** or **invertebrates**. Vertebrates can be placed in one of five **classes** — fish, amphibians, reptiles, birds and mammals.

a) What type of vertebrate do the following descriptions refer to?

i) They are cold blooded and breath through their permiable skin.

....

ii) They have scales, and gills for gas exchange. They live in water.

....

b) Describe the common features of vertebrates that are classsed as birds.

....

Q4 When scientists discovered the fossilised remains of the prehistoric animal ***Archaeopteryx***, they had some difficulty in **classifying** it. The animal had a structure that suggested wings and feathers, but also a long bony tail, clawed hands and sharp teeth like a lizard.

a) Why did the scientists have **difficulty** in classifying the *Archaeopteryx*?

....

b) Which features of the *Archaeopteryx* could be described as **reptilian**?

....

c) Do you think the *Archaeopteryx* would have **laid eggs**, or given birth to **live young**? Give a reason for your answer.

....

B1a Topic 1 — Environment

Changing Species' Characteristics

Q1 Humans have bred certain types of **cattle** to produce the largest possible **milk yields**.

a) Explain how this **selective breeding** can be done.

Select 2 animals with good characteristics breed them

b) Suggest one possible **disadvantage** of selective breeding.

it takes many generations (lots of time)

Q2 Give **two advantages** of using **genetic engineering** rather than selective breeding in developing new characteristics.

1. *Quicker*

2. *you can select exactly which characteristics you want*

Q3 **Tomato plants** are sensitive to **frost**. Scientists discovered a gene in some **fish** which enables them to survive extreme cold. Using **genetic engineering**, they inserted this gene into tomato plants to produce a new variety that is not killed by frost.

a) Suggest one **advantage** of developing frost-resistant tomatoes.

they are more likely to survive

b) Suggest one possible **disadvantage** of this procedure.

the characteristic could spread into other varietys of tomatoe plants

Q4 **Genetically modified** (GM) **crops** have been grown in trials in different parts of the UK. Laws have been passed to make sure that **no non-GM crops** are grown in a **'quarantine' zone** of several miles around the trial crops. Suggest why quarantine zones have been made compulsory.

so the characteristic can't spread

B1a Topic 1 — Environment

Human Activity and the Environment

Q1 The graph shows the amount of **sulphur dioxide** released in the UK between 1970 and 2003.

a) In which year shown on the graph were sulphur dioxide emissions **highest**?

...........1970...........

b) Approximately how much sulphur dioxide was emitted in 2003?

...........1m...........

c) Name one environmental **problem** caused by sulphur dioxide.

....

d) What process is mainly responsible for the sulphur dioxide emissions shown?

....

Q2 The graph shows the levels of **ozone** at different **heights** in the atmosphere. The black line shows the levels in **most parts of the world**, and the blue line shows the level over the **Antarctic circle**.

a) Which of the following would be the best **conclusion** from this data? Tick one box.

- [x] The levels of ozone are lowest over the Antarctic.
- [ ] CFCs are causing a hole in the ozone layer.
- [ ] Ozone levels are being depleted all over the world.

b) Why should we be **concerned** about a hole in the ozone layer?

...........global warming...........

....

c) How are **humans** contributing to the thinning of the ozone layer?

...........pollution...........

Q3 Huge numbers of **trees** are being **cut** or **burnt down** in the world's rainforests.

a) State **two** ways in which this deforestation may increase the problem of global warming.

1. ....burning produces carbon when burnt...........
2. ....less trees more carbon dioxide...........

b) State one other environmental problem resulting from deforestation.

....

B1a Topic 1 — Environment

Human Activity and the Environment

Q4 The size of the **Earth's population** has changed dramatically in the last 1000 years.

a) Use the table below to plot a graph on the grid, showing how the world's human population has changed over the last 1000 years.

NO. OF PEOPLE / BILLIONS	YEAR
0.3	1000
0.4	1200
0.4	1400
0.6	1600
1.0	1800
1.7	1900
6.1	2000

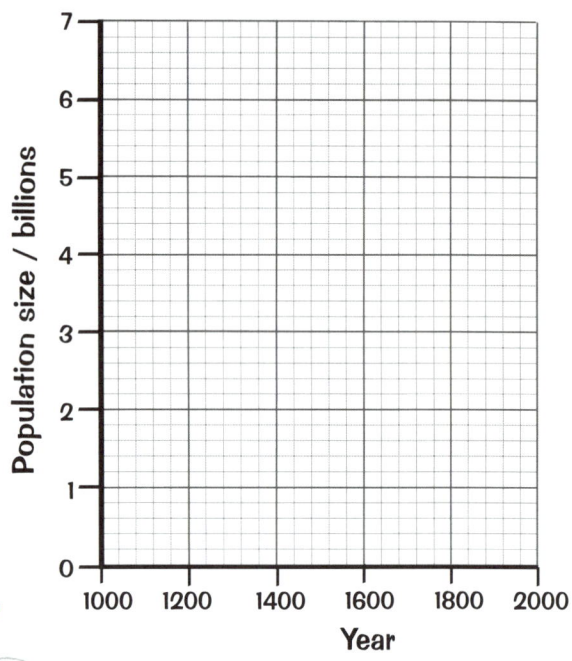

b) Circle the correct word to complete each sentence.

i) The size of the population now is **bigger** / smaller than it was 1000 years ago.

ii) The growth of the population now is slower / **faster** than it was 1000 years ago.

iii) The impact on the environment now is less / **greater** than it was 1000 years ago.

c) Suggest **two** reasons for the sudden increase in the population.

Civilisation / better standard of living

Q5 The size of **Earth's population** has an impact on our environment.

How would you expect an **increase** in population size to affect the following things? Explain your answers.

a) The amount of **raw materials** (including non-renewable energy resources)

they would decrease because everyone would want them

b) **Waste disposal**

increase more people would throw stuff away

c) **Greenhouse gas levels**

increase more people would be using things which emit them

B1a Topic 1 — Environment

Human Activity and the Environment

Q6 Suggest two reasons why, in general, **economically developed countries** cause more **pollution** than less developed countries.

1. ....
2. ....

Q7 The map shows the average levels of **sulphur dioxide pollution** in the air in the UK in 2000.

a) Which of the following is the best conclusion you could draw from this distribution? Tick one box.

☐ The pollution was worst in the north of the UK.

☐ The pollution came from factories.

☐ The pollution was worst in the middle of the UK.

☐ The pollution was a lot worse in 2000 than it was 100 years ago.

b) How would you expect the map to have looked **before** the Industrial Revolution? Explain why.

....

....

Q8 The graph shows the levels of **atmospheric carbon dioxide** between the years 1870 and 2000.

a) Estimate the date at which the atmospheric carbon dioxide level was at 320 ppm.

....

....

b) What are the main processes responsible for the increase in carbon dioxide levels?

....

c) Suggest **two** reasons why carbon dioxide emissions tend to increase as the people living in a country grow richer.

1. ....
2. ....

d) Suggest why a richer country might be better able to **reduce** its impact on the environment than a poorer country.

....

B1a Topic 1 — Environment

Human Activity and the Environment

Q9 In the list below, circle the letter(s) next to any factors that are likely to lead to an **increase** in the amount of **pollution** generated.

- A Industries developing and becoming more productive.
- B Farmers switching from modern to organic farming techniques.
- C Increases in the Earth's human population.
- D More widespread use of renewable energy resources.
- E Improvements in the overall standard of living of the Earth's human population.

Farmer Gideon had a brand new combine harvester and he wasn't going to give anyone the keys.

Q10 Over the last 10 years, much more **organic food** has appeared in British supermarkets. Organic farmers do not use **artificial pesticides** or **fertilisers**.

a) What do organic farmers use instead of artificial fertilisers?

....

b) How do organic farmers **control pests** without using chemical pesticides?

....

c) Organic farmers use **crop rotation** to help keep their soil fertile. Explain what this means.

....

....

d) Suggest two reasons why some people **prefer** to buy organic produce.

1. ....

2. ....

e) Organic products are **more expensive**. Explain why this is.

....

f) Suggest another reason why some people **do not** buy organic produce.

....

Top Tip: As countries become more economically developed, the people stop farming their own little plots and start manufacturing. This takes its toll on the environment, so they pass laws to protect it. Then they get so advanced that they all become lawyers and advertising executives and accountants instead, and do all their manufacturing in poorer countries with no environmental laws. Oh dear.

B1a Topic 1 — Environment

B1a Topic 2 — Genes

Variation in Plants and Animals

Q1 Complete this passage by circling the **best** word or phrase from each highlighted pair.

> Usually, organisms of the same species **have differences** / **are identical**.
> This is partly because different organisms have different **alleles** / **cells**, which
> they inherit from their parents. **Siblings** / **Identical twins** are exceptions to this.
> But even they usually have some different features, such as **hairstyle** / **eye colour**.
> These differences are due to their environment. The differences between
> individual organisms are known as **variation** / **inheritance**.

Q2 Helen and Stephanie are **identical twins**. Helen has dark hair and Stephanie is blonde.

  a) Do you think that these are Helen and Stephanie's **natural** hair colours? Explain your answer.

  ....

  ....

  b) Helen weighs 7 kg more than Stephanie. Say whether this is due to genes, environment or both, and explain your answer.

  ....

  ....

  c) Stephanie has a **birthmark** on her shoulder shaped like Wayne Rooney. Helen doesn't. Do you think birthmarks are caused by your genes? Explain why.

  ....

  ....

Q3 Human growth is controlled by genes, but is also affected by the environment.

  a) What effect does a **poor diet** have on growth?

  ....

  b) The graph on the right shows the variation in height with age for a well nourished child. Draw a line on the graph to represent a **malnourished** child.

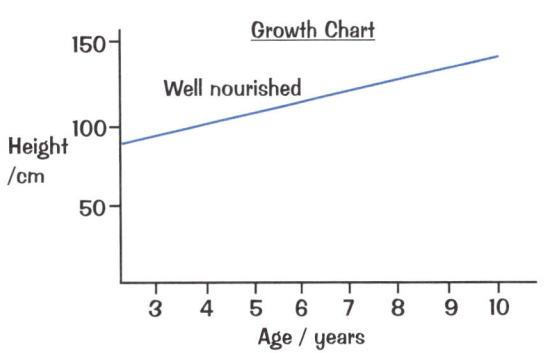

Variation in Plants and Animals

Q4 For each of these characteristics, say whether it depends on **genes**, the **environment** or **both**.

a) A person's blood group. .... *genes* ....

b) Someone being able to roll their tongue. .... *genes* ....

c) Someone having cystic fibrosis. .... *genes* ....

d) Someone knowing how to speak Spanish. .... *environment* ....

e) The colour of a plant's flowers. .... *both* ....

f) The height of a plant. .... *both* ....

Q5 Charlie did an experiment to examine the effect of **minerals** on the growth of **two species** of **wheat plant**. He took 60 seedlings of species 1, and divided them into six groups. He repeated this with species 2. He planted each group of seedlings in **identical pots of soil**, but gave them different concentrations of minerals. The table shows the results that Charlie got.

Concentration of mineral / ppm	Change in height of species 1 after 3 weeks / cm	Change in height of species 2 after 3 weeks / cm
0	0	0
100	2	12
200	6	21
300	15	29
400	17	34
500	21	40

a) Explain why Charlie used **ten** seedlings in each group, instead of just one.
  to make it a fair test (get average)

b) Charlie put all the seedlings into **identical pots** and used the **same type** of soil.

  i) Explain why he did this.
  to only vary 1 thing

  ii) Suggest **two** other things that Charlie should try to keep the same.
  temperature / water

c) What do Charlie's results suggest about the effect of minerals on the growth of these plants?
  more minerals the taller the plant

d) Do you think that the growth of Charlie's plants was affected by genes, the environment or both? Explain your answer.
  both a plant might have the gene to be tall but without nutrients wouldent be tall and vice versa

B1a Topic 2 — Genes

DNA and Genes

Q1 Complete the passage using some of the words given below.

DNA	nucleus	genes	chromosomes
membrane	allele	proteins	

Each cell of the body contains a structure called the ....

This structure contains strands of genetic information called ....

These strands are made of a chemical called ....

Sections of genetic material that control different characteristics are called ....

These are chemical instructions that determine what .... a cell makes.

Q2 Write out these structures in order of size, **starting with the smallest**.

| nucleus | gene | chromosome | cell |

1. .... 2. .... 3. .... 4. ....

Q3 Which of the following is the correct definition of the term '**alleles**'?
Circle the letter next to the correct answer.

A 'Alleles' is the collective term for all the genes found on a pair of chromosomes.

B 'Alleles' are different forms of the same gene.

C 'Alleles' are identical organisms produced by asexual reproduction.

Q4 Tick the correct boxes to show whether each statement is **true** or **false**.   True False

a) Human body cells contain 44 chromosomes.   ☐ ☐

b) Chromosomes are long lengths of DNA coiled up.   ☐ ☐

c) Human body cells contain two number 19 chromosomes.   ☐ ☐

d) All species have the same number of chromosomes.   ☐ ☐

Top Tip: DNA and genes are pretty important to understanding biology — they control everything a cell does and the characteristics that will be passed on from parents to kids. Make sure you know that genes control the proteins that are made, and the proteins control the cell.

B1a Topic 2 — Genes

Asexual Reproduction

Q1 Draw lines to match each of the terms below with its description.

- Asexual — genetically identical individuals
- Clones — type of cell division that produces genetically identical cells
- Mitosis — process used to produce new organisms
- Reproduction — type of reproduction where there is only one parent

Q2 Name two organisms that can **reproduce asexually**.

1. Strawberry plant
2. ~~ider~~ plant

Q3 **Diagram 1** shows a cell that is **about to divide** by **mitosis**. Two pairs of chromosomes are shown. Complete **Diagram 2** to show how the chromosomes would appear just before the cell has divided completely.

Diagram 1 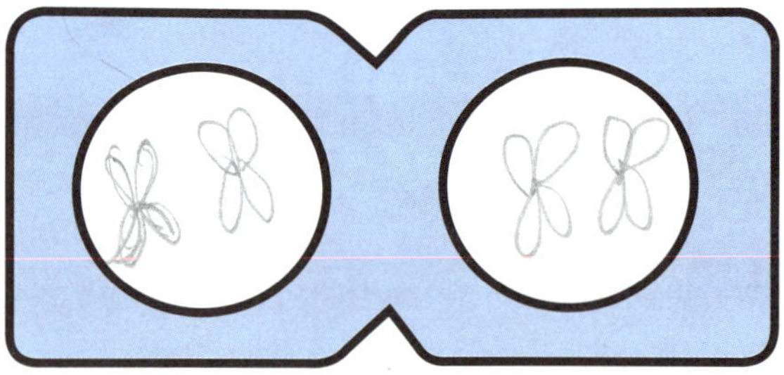   Diagram 2

Q4 Arrange these events in **mitosis** in the correct order by writing the correct number in each box.

- [ ] The DNA copies itself before it coils up and forms chromosomes.
- [ ] The DNA uncoils.
- [x] The chromosomes line up in the centre of the cell.
- [ ] New membranes form around the cell nuclei.
- [ ] The arms of each chromosome are pulled apart.
- [ ] The cell divides.

B1a Topic 2 — Genes

Sexual Reproduction and Variation

Q1 Circle the correct word(s) in each pair to complete the sentences below.

a) Sperm and egg cells are called **gametes** / zygotes.

b) The fusion, or joining, of sperm and egg cells is called **fertilisation** / mitosis.

c) When sperm and egg cells fuse, they produce a gamete / **zygote**.

d) A gamete contains chromosomes from **one parent** / both parents.

e) A zygote contains chromosomes from one parent / **both parents**.

f) Sexual reproduction leads to **more** / less genetic variation than asexual reproduction.

Q2 The body cells of a fruit fly contain **four pairs** of chromosomes. When **gametes** are formed, these pairs separate. Two of the four pairs of chromosomes are shown in the diagram below.

a) Draw the chromosomes in the cells to show the two different ways that the chromosomes could separate during the first step in the formation of gametes.

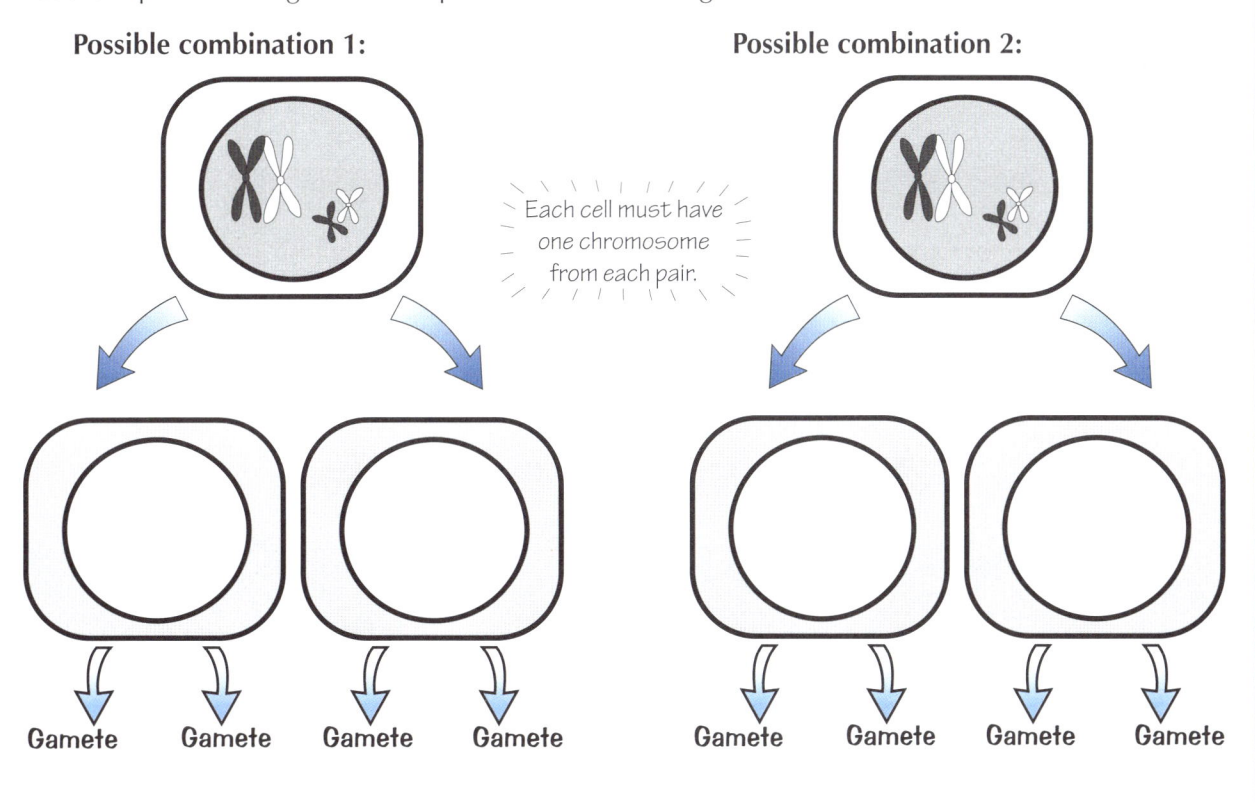

Possible combination 1:   **Possible combination 2:**

Each cell must have one chromosome from each pair.

Gamete   Gamete   Gamete   Gamete   Gamete   Gamete   Gamete   Gamete

b) Give the reason why gametes have **half** the usual number of chromosomes.

....

....

c) Explain how gamete formation **leads to genetic variation**.

....

....

B1a Topic 2 — Genes

Sexual Reproduction and Variation

Q3 The diagram shows human **sperm** and **egg** cells combining, and the **fertilised egg** cell dividing. Write numbers on the nuclei of each cell to show how many **chromosomes** each contains.

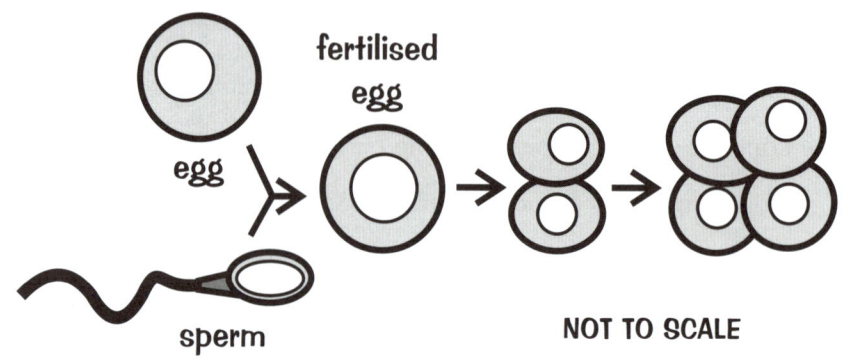

egg → *fertilised egg* → →

sperm

NOT TO SCALE

Q4 **Fertilisation** is the fusion of male and female gametes to form a zygote. Explain how the process of fertilisation **leads to genetic variation**.

....

....

....

Q5 Mr O'Riley breeds **racehorses**. He breeds his best black racing stallion, Snowball, with his best black racing mare, Goldie.

Why is there no guarantee that any foal born will be a champion racer?

....

....

Q6 Tick the correct boxes to show whether the following statements are **true** or **false**.

		True	False
a)	Mutations are always harmful.	☐	☐
b)	Mutations can occur spontaneously.	☐	☐
c)	Mutations can prevent the production of a protein.	☐	☐
d)	Mutations occurring in body cells are passed on to offspring.	☐	☐
e)	Cigarette smoke contains mutagens.	☐	☐
f)	Mutations cause genetic variation.	☐	☐

B1a Topic 2 — Genes

Genetic Diagrams

Q1 Match each of the terms below with its meaning.

- **dominant** — having two different alleles for a gene
- **genotype** — having two identical alleles for a gene
- **heterozygous** — expressed in organisms heterozygous for that trait
- **homozygous** — not expressed in organisms heterozygous for that trait
- **phenotype** — the expressed characteristics of an individual
- **recessive** — the genes that an individual contains

Q2 Wilma carries a **recessive** allele for **red** hair and a **dominant** allele for **brown** hair.

a) What is Wilma's natural hair colour?

....

b) Is Wilma homozygous or heterozygous for this characteristic?

....

Q3 Fruit flies usually have **red** eyes. However, there are a small number of white-eyed fruit flies. Having **white** eyes is a **recessive** characteristic.

a) Complete the following sentences with either '**red eyes**' or '**white eyes**'.

i) **R** is the allele for ....

ii) **r** is the allele for ....

iii) Fruit flies with alleles **RR** or **Rr** will have ....

iv) Fruit flies with the alleles **rr** will have ....

b) Two fruit flies have the alleles **Rr**. They fall in love and get it on.

i) Complete this genetic diagram to show the possible offspring. One's been done for you.

parent's alleles

	R	r
R	RR	
r		

parent's alleles

Read up and across to work out what combination of alleles should be in each box.

ii) What is the probability that the fruit flies' offspring will have **white eyes**?

....

iii) The fruit flies have 16 offspring. How many of the offspring are **likely** to have **red eyes**?

....

B1a Topic 2 — Genes

Genetic Diagrams

Q4 The **seeds** of pea plants can be **smooth** or **wrinkled**. The allele for smooth seeds (**S**) is dominant. The allele for wrinkled seeds (**s**) is recessive.

a) Complete the genetic diagram below. It shows a cross between a homozygous smooth seed pea plant (genotype **SS**) and a homozygous wrinkled seed pea plant (genotype **ss**).

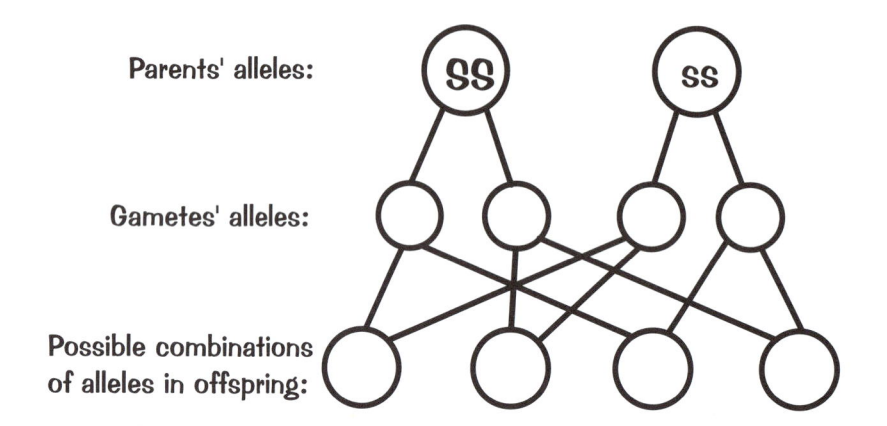

Parents' alleles: SS   ss

Gametes' alleles: ○ ○ ○ ○

Possible combinations of alleles in offspring: ○ ○ ○ ○

b) In this cross, what is the probability that any one of the offspring will have wrinkled seeds? Tick the correct option.

☐ 100% chance of being wrinkled.
☐ 50% chance of being wrinkled.
☐ 25% chance of being wrinkled.
☐ 0% chance of being wrinkled.

Pictures of peas are very dull. So here's a picture of Elvis instead.

c) Complete the genetic diagram below to show the possible combinations of alleles in the offspring.

	parent's alleles	
	S	s
S		
s		

parent's alleles

d) Mrs Maguire crosses two pea plants with the alleles Ss. Is the following statement **true** or **false**? Tick the correct box.

"If Mrs Maguire gets 12 new seedlings as a result of her cross, the most likely number of seedlings with wrinkled seeds will be 3."

True ☐   False ☐

Top Tip: Lots of people prefer the grid-type genetic diagrams, but don't be scared of the ones with the blobs and lines. They look like a crazy mess at first but they're actually dead simple — every one of the four offspring circles must have **one letter** from **each** parent, **never** two from the same parent.

B1a Topic 2 — Genes

The Human Genome Project

Q1 Decide whether the following statements about the **human genome** are **true** or **false**.

                                                                                             True False

  a) The aim of the Human Genome Project was to find all of the 25 000 or so human genes. ☐ ☐

  b) Humans have 23 pairs of chromosomes. ☐ ☐

  c) Scientists now know the function of every one of the human genes. ☐ ☐

Q2 The Human Genome Project could lead to big improvements in **medical treatment**.

  a) Explain how information about a person's genes could be used to **prevent** diseases.

      ....

      ....

  b) Explain how information about a person's genes could be used to **treat** diseases.

      ....

      ....

Q3 Soon it may be possible to test a person's DNA to find out if they are likely to suffer from heart disease. Marco's genotype makes it likely that he will suffer from **heart disease** at an early age. Explain how it could have a **negative effect** on Marco if this fact was made available to:

  a) an **employer** who was about to offer him a job.

      ....

  b) an **insurance company** who were about to give him life insurance.

      ....

  c) Marco himself.

      ....

Q4 Police investigators can analyse DNA samples taken from the scene of a **crime** and compare this to the DNA of a **suspect**. In the future, it may be possible to look at the DNA samples from the crime scene and work out from them what the suspect **looks like**.

  a) Underline any of the following characteristics that could be deduced from a person's DNA.

      i) whether they have blue or brown eyes.   **ii)** whether they have a scar on their cheek.

      iii) whether they are male or female.   **iv)** whether they are fat or thin.

  b) Explain **why** some characteristics could be worked out from the DNA, but others could not.

      ....

      ....

B1a Topic 2 — Genes

Genetic Engineering

Q1 Explain how **genetic engineering** can be used to produce a lot of **human insulin** in a short time.

....

....

Q2 Put the following stages in the production of a **transgenic mouse** in the **correct order**.

- **A** A fertilised mouse's egg is implanted into the uterus of a living mouse.
- **B** A transgenic animal develops inside a surrogate mother.
- **C** An extract of DNA is taken from a human cell.
- **D** DNA is injected into a fertilised mouse's egg. **Order:** ....

Q3 A **goat** was developed from an egg that had had a **human gene** injected into it. The goat now produces a **human protein** in its milk. This protein is useful in treating people with haemophilia.

a) Explain why the goat is described as a **transgenic organism**.

....

b) Give one **advantage** of using a goat to obtain the protein, rather than genetically modified bacteria.

....

c) Some people **think** that it is **wrong** to use genetically engineered animals in this way. Explain why it might be thought wrong, from the point of view of:

i) animal welfare.

....

ii) the safety of haemophilia patients.

....

Q4 During *in vitro* fertilisation (IVF) a cell can be removed from an embryo and **screened** for **genetic disorders** like Huntington's disease. If a faulty allele is found, the embryo can be destroyed.

a) Explain why some people think embryo screening is a **bad** thing.

....

....

b) Explain why some people think embryo screening is a **good** thing.

....

....

B1a Topic 2 — Genes

Genetic Disorders and Gene Therapy

Q1 Circle the correct word in each pair to complete the sentences below.

a) Some alleles cause diseases that **can** / **can't** be inherited.

b) Gene therapy works by inserting a functioning **allele** / **chromosome** into the affected cells.

c) Gene therapy aims to treat the **symptoms** / **causes** of a disease. It can already be used to provide a **temporary** / **permanent** cure for some diseases, and there are high hopes for its future potential.

Q2 Billy has **cystic fibrosis**, an inherited genetic disorder caused by a **recessive allele**.

a) Say briefly how gene therapy could be used to help him.

....

....

b) Name one other genetic disorder caused by inheriting faulty alleles.

....

Q3 Decide whether each of the following statements is **true** or **false**.

		True	False
a)	Cystic fibrosis causes problems with the respiratory and digestive systems.	☐	☐
b)	Some people have genes that make them more likely to get cancer.	☐	☐
c)	Physiotherapy may one day form a permanent cure for cystic fibrosis.	☐	☐
d)	A tumour is caused by cells dividing and growing out of control.	☐	☐
e)	A person who has had gene therapy has no risk of developing cancer.	☐	☐

Q4 **Cancers** such as some types of breast cancer often **run in families**.

a) Explain what this shows about the disease.

....

....

b) In the future, it may be possible to alter the genes of an adult to make it less likely that they will suffer from breast cancer. However, this therapy is at an earlier stage of development than gene therapy for cystic fibrosis is. Suggest two reasons why the breast cancer therapy is taking **longer to develop**.

....

....

c) If a patient was treated using gene therapy to reduce their chances of getting breast cancer, might this genetic benefit be passed on to any children they had later? Explain your answer.

....

....

B1a Topic 2 — Genes

Cloning

Q1 Draw lines to match each of the '**cloning terms**' below with its meaning.

- clone — a developing fertilised egg
- enucleation — organism that is genetically identical to another
- embryo — removal of the nucleus from a cell

Q2 The diagram shows the **procedure** that can be used to **clone** a sheep.

a) Which of the labelled cells in the diagram are genetically identical to each other? Explain your answer.

....
....
....

b) Which of the sheep (X, Y or Z) will the clone be genetically identical to, and why?

....
....
....

c) When the embryo stage is reached in this process, it is possible to divide up the embryo cells, and implant different cells into different surrogates. What would be the effect of doing this?

....

d) In normal sexual reproduction, fertilisation is the fusion of the female and male gametes and their genetic material. Explain the difference between this process and cloning.

....
....
....

B1a Topic 2 — Genes

Cloning

Q3 There are two main types of cloning — **reproductive** and **therapeutic**. Decide whether each of these statements applies to reproductive cloning, therapeutic cloning or both.

a) Produces genetically identical cells. ....

b) Depends upon cells dividing by mitosis. ....

c) Clones are allowed to grow into a whole organism. ....

d) May be used in growing organs for transplant. ....

e) Clones develop from embryonic stem cells. ....

Q4 Discuss the **ethical** issues involved in using **embryonic stem cells** to treat diseases.

....

....

....

....

Q5 Cloning technology could prove **beneficial** in a number of ways.

a) Explain the reason for carrying out each of these possible procedures:

   i) Reproductive cloning of a sheep with particularly good quality wool.

   ....

   ii) Embryonic stem cells are used to grow a human heart.

   ....

   iii) Making a cloned embryo of a liver patient then extracting embryonic stem cells.

   ....

b) Many different animals have been cloned using reproductive cloning. It has not yet been done with a human and many people think it never should be. Explain the reasons behind this opinion.

....

....

....

Top Tip: Hmmm, cloning. It's **always** in the news, with various mad scientists regularly claiming to be about to clone the first human. You have to take this type of story with a pinch of salt though, because the media often aren't too keen on letting the **facts** get in the way of a **good story**.

B1a Topic 2 — Genes

Mixed Questions — B1a Topics 1 & 2

Q1 In the Arctic, the **lemming** is prey for the **Arctic fox**.

   a) The Arctic fox is adapted for the cold Arctic conditions, e.g. it has thick white fur for insulation and camouflage. Explain how **natural selection** has led to adaptations such as these becoming widespread in the Arctic fox population.

   ....

   ....

   b) The food chain is: **vegetation → lemmings → Arctic fox**

   i) In the box, sketch a **pyramid of biomass** for the food chain.

   ii) Suggest two factors that could cause the Arctic fox population to decrease.

   ....

   ....

   iii) Why won't all the energy that the lemmings gain from the vegetation be passed to the fox?

   ....

   ....

   c) Use the **binomial system** to write down the scientific name of the Arctic fox (order *Carnivora*, family *Canidae*, genus *Alopex*, species *lagopus*).

   ....

Q2 Both the **human population** and the global level of **development** are increasing rapidly.

   a) These changes are affecting the environment.
   Explain how the release of CFCs is damaging the environment.

   ....

   ....

   b) Give **two** other ways that the increasing human population is negatively affecting the environment.

   1. ....

   2. ....

   c) Many people believe that converting from intensive farming to **organic farming** is one way we can **reduce** our impact on the environment. Outline the principles of organic farming.

   ....

   ....

B1a Topic 2 — Genes

Mixed Questions — B1a Topics 1 & 2

Q3 Fiona says, "**All** organisms contain some **DNA** from their **father** and some DNA from their **mother**."

a) Explain why Fiona's statement is **incorrect**, including an example.
....
....

b) Clones are genetically identical organisms. Outline one **ethical** concern with cloning mammals.
....

c) Explain why organisms that reproduce **sexually** contain DNA from both their parents.
....
....

Q4 Mr and Mrs Carlton are both carriers of **cystic fibrosis** (CF), a **recessive** genetic disorder.

a) Mr and Mrs Carlton are planning a family. Complete the genetic diagram to show the probability of one of their children suffering from the disorder. Use the symbols **C** and **c** to represent the alleles.

b) What is the probability of the child being a CF sufferer? ....

c) Explain how using **IVF** can help to reduce the number of people with CF.
....
....
....

Q5 The **characteristics** of a **species** may **change** over time.

a) Fill in this table using the entries provided.

Genetic engineering   None   Within a generation   Several generations   Partial

Mechanism of change	Amount of **human** control	Time taken for a **useful** change to occur
Selective breeding		
	Full	

b) Give **one** reason why **Darwin** experienced difficulty getting his theory of evolution accepted.
....

B1a Topic 2 — Genes

The Nervous System

Q1 Complete the following passage by choosing the correct words from the box.

~~brain~~ ~~synapses~~ ~~peripheral~~ ~~central~~ ~~motor~~ ~~glands~~
~~effectors~~ ~~spinal~~ ~~chemical~~ ~~electrical~~ ~~sensory~~

The *Central* nervous system refers to all neurones found in the *brain* and *Spinal* cord. All the other neurones in the body make up the *Sensory* nervous system. Neurones transmit *Electrical* [written over *chemical*] impulses from sense organs to the CNS along *motor* neurones. Impulses from the CNS are sent along *peripheral* neurones to *effectors*, which are muscles or *glands*. There are gaps between neurones called *Synapses* — the impulse is transmitted from one neurone to another by *Chemical* transmitters.

Q2 Which of the following is **not** an example of a **stimulus**? Underline your answer.

pressure   <u>chemical</u>   hearing   change in body position   change in temperature

Q3 In each sentence below, underline the **sense organ** involved and write down the **type of receptor** that is detecting the stimulus.

a) Tariq puts a piece of lemon on his <u>tongue</u>. The lemon tastes sour.
   taste

b) Siobhan wrinkles her nose as she smells something unpleasant in her baby brother's nappy.
   ....

c) Lindsey covers her eyes when she sees the man in the mask jump out during a scary film.
   ....

Q4 Give two reasons why it is important for animals to be able to **detect changes** in their surroundings.

....
....

Q5 Explain why a man with a **damaged spinal cord** may not be able to feel someone touching his toe.

....
....

The Nervous System

Q6 Some parts of the body are known as the **CNS**.

a) What do the letters **CNS** stand for? ....

b) Name the two main parts of the CNS.

1. ......spine...... 2. ......brain......

c) What type of neurone:

i) carries information **to** the CNS? ......sensory......

ii) carries instructions **from** the CNS? ......motor neurone......

Q7 John and Marc investigated how **sensitive** different parts of the body are to **pressure**. They stuck two pins in a cork 0.5 cm apart. The pins were placed on different parts of the body. Ten pupils took part — they were blindfolded and reported "yes" or "no" to feeling both points. The results of the experiment are shown in the table.

Area of the body tested	Number of pupils reporting 'yes'
Sole of foot	2
Knee	3
Fingertip	10
Back of hand	5
Lip	9

a) Which part of the body do the results suggest is:

i) most sensitive? .... ii) least sensitive? ....

b) From the results above, which part of the body do you think contains the greatest concentration of **pressure receptors**? Explain your answer.

....

....

c) John and Marc took it in turns to test the pupils. Their teacher suggested that if only one of the boys had done all the testing, the experiment would have been fairer. Explain why.

....

....

d) Each pupil was tested once. Suggest how you might make the test more accurate.

....

....

B1b Topic 3 — Electrical & Chemical Signals

The Central Nervous System

Q1 Decide whether each of the statements below is **true** or **false**.

		True	False
a)	The right side of the cerebrum controls the left side of the body.	☐	☐
b)	The cerebellum is the largest part of the brain.	☐	☐
c)	Each sense (sight, hearing etc.) is processed in a different area (or areas) of the brain.	☐	☐
d)	The cerebrum coordinates sensory information.	☐	☐

Q2 Complete the passage below about **Parkinson's disease** by circling the correct words in each pair.

> Parkinson's disease is due to a loss of neurones / blood supply in the area of the brain which controls thinking / movement. It can often result in people having fits / shaking uncontrollably. There are drugs available which can be used to control / cure the disease.

Q3 Look at the graph showing **death rates** from **strokes** for people in the UK aged 65–74 between 1970 and 2002.

a) Which of the following would be the **best** conclusion from the above data? Tick **one** box.

☐ **A** Strokes used to be more common than they are now.

☐ **B** Strokes are a major cause of death in the developed world.

☐ **C** The death rate from strokes for people aged 65 to 74 has steadily declined since 1970.

☐ **D** Most people who die from strokes are aged between 65–74.

b) What is the usual cause of a stroke?

....

....

> **Top Tips:** An adult human brain weighs about 1.4 kg — it's an incredibly complicated system of about 100 billion nerves, and if you could unravel them all, they'd stretch to more than 150 000 km. You don't need to know any of that, but I reckon it's pretty interesting stuff...

B1b Topic 3 — Electrical & Chemical Signals

The Central Nervous System

Q4 Brain tumours have different symptoms depending on their size and their location.

a) How is a brain tumour formed?
....

b) What is the difference between a cancerous (malignant) brain tumour and a benign one?
....

c) State two ways in which a brain tumour may be treated.
....

Q5 Epilepsy is a disorder of the brain.

a) State two possible causes of epilepsy.
....

b) What happens to someone with grand mal epilepsy when they have an epileptic seizure?
....

Epileptic seizures can sometimes be brought on when people with epilepsy watch TV. Scientists did an experiment to see if the size of the patient's TV set made any difference to the likelihood of it causing a seizure. The results are shown in the table on the right.

Size of TV screen (inches)	Percentage of patients reporting a seizure
14	12
17	17
24	25
28	27
32	33

c) What conclusion could be drawn from these results?
....

d) The scientists carrying out the experiment could not ensure a completely fair test. State whether each factor described below could make their data unreliable and explain your answer.

i) The TVs used were not all placed on the same type of table as they were watched.
....
....

ii) The age range was not the same for every group (e.g. the patients with the 14-inch TVs ranged from age 15 to 33, whereas those with the 32-inch TVs ranged from age 15 to 72).
....
....

B1b Topic 3 — Electrical & Chemical Signals

Voluntary and Reflex Responses

Q1 Circle the correct answers to complete the following sentences.

a) Reflexes happen more **quickly** / **slowly** than considered responses.

b) The **vertebrae** / **spinal cord** can coordinate a reflex response.

c) The main purpose of a reflex is to **protect** / **display** the body.

d) Reflexes happen **with** / **without** conscious thought.

Q2 Explain what a **reflex arc** is.

....
....
....
....
....

Q3 Explain why a **reflex** reaction is faster than a **voluntary** reaction.

Think about where the impulse has to go to.

....
....
....

Q4 **Swallowing** is a **reflex**, yet you also seem to be able to do it on purpose. However, if you try to swallow twice in quick succession, it is impossible. The only time that you can do it is when you are **drinking**.

Suggest an explanation for why you can swallow several times in succession when you are drinking, but only once when you are not.

Think about what sets off a reflex.

....
....
....
....

Top Tips: Reflexes are really fast — that's the whole point of them. And the fewer synapses the signals have to cross, the faster the reaction. Doctors test people's reflexes by tapping below their knees to make their legs jerk. This reflex takes less than 50 milliseconds as only two synapses are involved.

B1b Topic 3 — Electrical & Chemical Signals

Voluntary and Reflex Responses

Q5 When you touch something hot with a finger you **automatically** pull the finger away. The diagram shows some parts of the nervous system involved in this **reflex action**.

a) What type of neurone is:

   i) neurone **X**? ....

   ii) neurone **Y**? ....

   iii) neurone **Z**? ....

b) Complete the sentence.

   In this reflex action the muscle acts as the ....

Q6 Tom and Jane did an experiment on **reaction times**. Tom held a ruler vertically between Jane's thumb and forefinger, with her forefinger in line with the zero mark. Tom dropped the ruler **without warning** and measured how far it fell before Jane caught it. They repeated their experiment three times. The three measurements (**in cm**) were **15**, **28** and **8**.

Tom holds the ruler between Jane's thumb and forefinger.

He lets go of the ruler.

Jane catches it as soon as she can.

a) Suggest two reasons why the results varied so much.

   1. ....

   2. ....

b) Tom and Jane's teacher said that they needed to repeat their experiment at least 10 times. Why did she suggest so many repeats?

   ....

   ....

B1b Topic 3 — Electrical & Chemical Signals

Examples of Reflex Actions

Q1 From the list below, underline any actions that are examples of **reflex actions**.

Pupil getting smaller in bright light

Catching a ball that is thrown to you

Pulling your hand away from something hot

Sneezing

Wiping a piece of dirt from your eye

Blinking when something flies at your face

Q2 Look carefully at the diagrams showing two different **eyes** below.

Eye A   Eye B — pupil, iris

a) Which diagram shows an eye in bright light? Explain your answer.

....

....

b) Explain the advantage of having a reflex response controlling the action of the iris.

....

....

Q3 Read the following passage about accommodation and circle the correct word in each pair.

When you look at objects, **light / distance** receptors send a message along a **motor / sensory** neurone to your brain. Your brain works out if the object is in focus and if it's not it sends a message along a **motor / sensory** neurone to the ciliary muscles, which control the thickness of the lens. If the object is far away, the ciliary muscles **contract / relax**, and the suspensory ligaments **tighten / slacken**. The lens will be **thin / fat**. The opposite happens for near objects.

Q4 Read the passage below and then answer the questions.

'Ducking' when an object flies at your head is an example of a reflex action. The eyes detect an object approaching at speed and send a signal to the brain. The brain immediately sends a signal back out to the various muscles that need to contract in order to move the head out of the way.

a) What sort of neurone carries the signal from the eyes to the brain? ....

b) From the passage, identify the following:
   i) The stimulus .... ii) The receptor ....
   iii) The effectors .... iv) The response ....

B1b Topic 3 — Electrical & Chemical Signals

The Blood

Q1 Which of these statements are **true** and which are **false**? Tick the correct boxes. True False

a) The main function of red blood cells is to fight germs. ☐ ☐

b) A higher than normal white blood cell count means you're more likely to get an infection. ☐ ☐

c) Glucose can be found in the blood. ☐ ☐

d) The liquid part of blood is called urea. ☐ ☐

e) Platelets seal wounds to prevent blood loss. ☐ ☐

Q2 **Red blood cells** carry **oxygen** in the blood.

a) i) Name the substance in these cells that combines with oxygen. ....

ii) Name the substance created when oxygen joins with this substance. ....

b) Red blood cells are replaced roughly every 120 days. Approximately how many times per year are all the red blood cells in the body replaced? ....

Q3 **White blood cells** defend the body against **disease**.

a) State three ways in which white blood cells can protect your body from microorganisms.

1. ....

2. ....

3. ....

b) A man was feeling unwell and went to see his doctor. The doctor did a blood test and found that the patient's white blood cell count was higher than normal. Suggest a reason for this.

....

Q4 **Plasma** is the substance that carries everything in the blood.

a) List six substances that are carried by **plasma**.

....

....

b) For each of the substances listed in the table, state where in the body it is travelling **from** and **to**.

Substance	Travelling from	Travelling to
Urea		
Carbon dioxide		
Glucose		

B1b Topic 3 — Electrical & Chemical Signals

Hormones

Q1 Complete the passage below about **hormones**.

> Hormones are .... messengers. They are produced in .... and released into the .... They are carried all around the body, but only affect certain .... cells.

Q2 Hormones can reach **every cell** in the body. Explain why only the **target cells** respond to the hormone while the others are unaffected.

....

....

Q3 One of the first experiments to show hormones working was done by two scientists called Bayliss and Starling. They knew that the presence of **food** in the **stomach** caused the **pancreas** (a completely different organ) to produce pancreatic juice, but they didn't know if the pancreas was triggered by **nerves** or by something in the **blood**.

  a) When they sedated a dog and cut away all the **nerves** going to the stomach and pancreas, pancreatic juice was still produced. Underline the best conclusion based on these findings.

  Nerves control the production of pancreatic juice.

  The stimulus which causes pancreatic juice to be made is carried in the blood.

  b) Next, they extracted some fluid from the dog's **stomach lining** and injected it into its **bloodstream**. Pancreatic juice was produced again. Underline the best conclusion based on these findings.

  A chemical produced by the stomach lining plays some part in pancreatic juice production.

  Something in food causes pancreatic juice to be produced.

Q4 Complete the table below showing **hormones**, where they are **produced** and the **action** they have.

HORMONE	SITE OF PRODUCTION	ACTION
Insulin		
		Helps control the menstrual cycle
Progesterone		

Q5 Describe the major differences between responses brought about by **hormones** and those due to the **nervous system**.

....

....

....

B1b Topic 3 — Electrical & Chemical Signals

Hormones — Insulin and Diabetes

Q1 The amount of **sugar** in the **blood** must be carefully controlled.

a) Where does the sugar in your blood come from?

....

b) Name the **two** main organs that are involved in the control of blood sugar levels.

....

c) Name a hormone involved in the regulation of blood sugar levels.

....

Q2 Deepa doesn't eat anything for lunch because she is busy. At **3pm** she has two biscuits and by **6pm** she is so hungry that for tea she eats a plate of pasta and six slices of toast with jam. Sketch a **line graph** showing Deepa's blood sugar levels from **12pm** to **8pm** on the axes below.

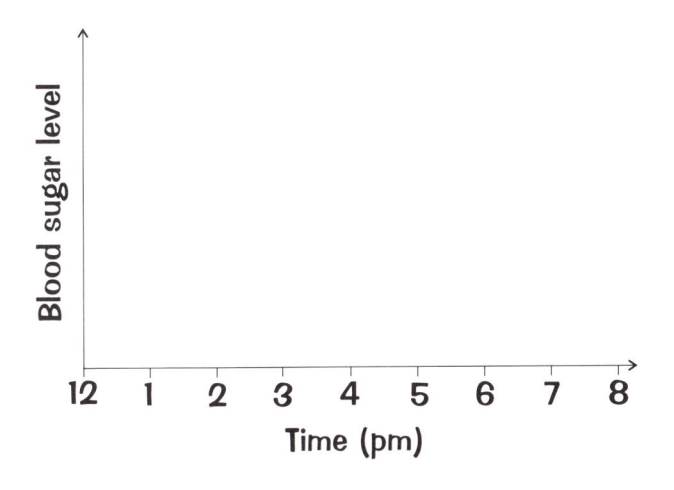

Q3 Approximately **1.8 million** people in the UK have **diabetes**.

a) Explain what type 1 diabetes is.

....

....

b) Which organ starts to remove glucose from the blood when insulin is injected by a type 1 diabetic?

....

Top Tips: Although diabetes is a serious disease, many diabetics are able to control their blood sugar levels and carry on with their normal lives. Sir Steve Redgrave even won a gold medal at the Olympics after he had been diagnosed with diabetes.

B1b Topic 3 — Electrical & Chemical Signals

Hormones — Insulin and Diabetes

Q4 Ruby and Paul both have diabetes and need to **monitor** and **control** their glucose levels carefully.

a) Describe the two main ways that diabetics can **control** their blood sugar levels

1. ....

2. ....

b) Ruby injects insulin just before she is about to eat a big meal. However, she has to go out at short notice and doesn't get time to eat. A few hours later, Ruby faints. Explain why this happens.

....

....

....

c) One evening Paul goes out for a meal. He has forgotten to inject any insulin, and eats a large meal including a sugary desert. A few hours after the meal Paul collapses and has to be taken to hospital for treatment.

i) Explain why Paul collapsed.

....

....

....

ii) What treatment would you expect Paul to be given when he arrives at hospital?

....

....

Q5 Diabetics used to inject themselves with insulin that came from **cows** and **pigs**. Nowadays, all the insulin used is human insulin, which is made by **genetically modified bacteria**.

a) How are the bacteria modified so that they produce human insulin?

....

....

b) Give two advantages of using human insulin produced by bacteria rather than cow or pig insulin.

1. ....

2. ....

B1b Topic 3 — Electrical & Chemical Signals

Hormones — The Menstrual Cycle

Q1 These diagrams show some events in the **menstrual cycle**. Put the events in the order in which they happen by writing numbers in the boxes, and then describe each event **briefly**.

Don't forget, the cycle begins with the first day of a period.

☐ ....
....
....

☐ ....
....
....

☐ ....
....
....

'Uterus' is the biological word for the 'womb'.

Q2 An **egg** is usually released on about **day 14** of the menstrual cycle.

a) Why does the uterus wall become thick and spongy before the egg is released?
....
....

b) Explain why there are only a few days in each menstrual cycle when fertilisation can take place.
....
....

c) What happens in the uterus if the egg is not fertilised?
....
....

B1b Topic 3 — Electrical & Chemical Signals

Hormones — The Menstrual Cycle

Q3 Listed below are some effects of **hormones** in females. Name each of the hormones involved.

a) Causes the lining of the uterus to thicken. ....

b) Maintains the lining of the uterus. ....

c) Stimulates egg release. ....

Q4 Normally, the levels of **progesterone** in a woman's body go up and down during each month. During **pregnancy**, however, the level remains **constant**. Why is this important for pregnancy to be successful?

....

....

Q5 The diagram below shows the ways in which **levels of hormones** and the **uterus lining** change during the **menstrual cycle**.

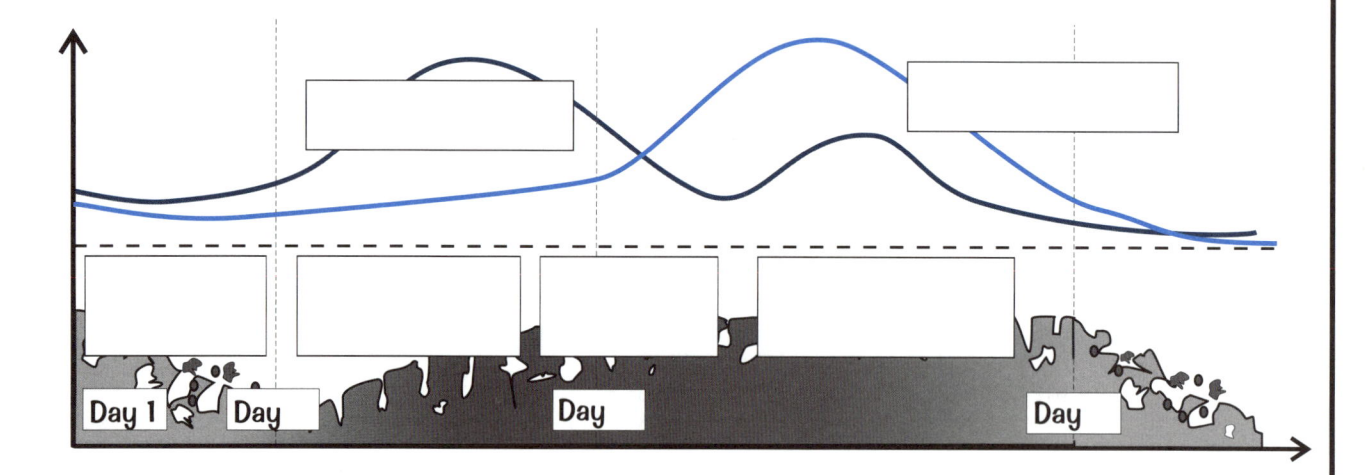

a) Fill in the day numbers in the boxes where they are missing.

b) Fill in the remaining boxes using the labels below:

Uterus lining builds up   Progesterone   Egg released

Oestrogen   Uterus lining maintained   Uterus lining breaks down

Top Tips: Sometimes, it's haaard to be... a womaaan... Or a man for that matter, if you're trying to learn about the menstrual cycle. This isn't really a topic where your natural intelligence and deep understanding of science can shine through much — you've just got to get your head down and learn the four stages and what each hormone does. Sorry.

B1b Topic 3 — Electrical & Chemical Signals

Hormones — Fertility

Q1 **The pill** is an **oral contraceptive** that contains oestrogen and progesterone. Explain how it is used to reduce fertility.

....

....

Q2 Hormones can also be used to **increase fertility**.

a) Name the hormone often taken by women who aren't releasing any eggs. ....

b) Describe two possible disadvantages of taking hormones to increase fertility in women.

....

....

Q3 **In vitro fertilisation** can help couples to have children.

a) Explain how **in vitro fertilisation** works.

....

....

b) Discuss the advantages and disadvantages of in vitro fertilisation.

....

....

....

Image based on data produced by the Human Fertilisation and Embryology Authority: www.hfea.gov.uk

Q4 The graph shows the **percentage success rates** of **IVF treatment** for women in the UK in 2002–3.

a) What was the % success rate in women aged 35–37? ....

b) What conclusion can be drawn about the effect of a woman's age on the success of IVF treatment?

....

....

c) IVF treatment is expensive, but for some couples the costs are paid by the National Health Service. From the graph and your own knowledge, suggest two reasons why the NHS might decide not to pay for IVF treatment for women over 40.

....

....

B1b Topic 3 — Electrical & Chemical Signals

The Body's Defence Systems

Q1 The body has several methods of **defending itself** against the entry of **pathogens**.

  a) Below are examples of how some bacterial pathogens can enter the body. In each case, describe how your body prevents against illness.

  i) *Staphylococcus aureus* can cause blood poisoning by getting into the blood through cuts.

  ....

  ii) *Streptococcus pneumoniae* can enter the body from the air as a person breathes.

  ....

  b) Explain how the sensitive eye area is protected against infection by microorganisms.

  ....

Q2 **Lymphocytes** and **phagocytes** are two different types of **white blood cell** that defend the body against invasion by microorganisms.

  a) Decide whether each of the following sentences applies to **lymphocytes**, to **phagocytes** or to **both**.

  i) They are able to kill invading microbes directly. ....

  ii) They are non-specific and attack any 'foreign' bodies. ....

  iii) They are able to secrete antibodies. ....

  iv) They have receptors which allow them to attack specific microbes. ....

  b) White blood cells also trigger an **inflammatory response**. Describe the effect that this has on the body, and explain why it is necessary.

  ....

  ....

  ....

Q3 Circle the correct word from each pair to complete the following passage.

Lymphocytes have receptors that allow them to recognise molecules called **antibodies** / **antigens** on the surface of certain **phagocytes** / **pathogens**. Some types of lymphocyte secrete **antibodies** / **antigens** that latch onto the invading cells and mark them so that other white blood cells can recognise and kill them. Other types attach directly to **antigens** / **antibodies** and destroy the cell carrying it.

Q4 If you have already had chickenpox you will usually be **immune** to the disease and will not suffer any symptoms if you are exposed to the infection again. Explain why this is.

....

....

....

Infectious Diseases

Q1 **Infectious diseases** are caused by **pathogens**.
Decide whether the following statements are **true** or **false**.

	True	False
a) All pathogens are parasites.	☐	☐
b) Infectious diseases can be passed on genetically.	☐	☐
c) All pathogens are bacteria.	☐	☐
d) Infectious diseases are not caused by living organisms.	☐	☐
e) Pathogens can be spread between organisms by both direct and indirect contact.	☐	☐

Q2 Some infectious diseases are spread by **direct contact**.

a) Explain what this means.

....

....

....

b) The table below shows ways that infections can be passed on. In each case, give one **example** of a disease that might be spread in this way, and say whether it is an example of **vertical** transmission or **horizontal** transmission.

	Droplet infection	Placental infection (from mother to baby)	Sexually transmitted infection
Example			
Type of transmission			

Q3 Complete the following passage by circling the correct words.

> **Influenza** is spread by **vertical transmission / droplet infection** — in the same way as **TB / rabies**. It's transmitted when an infected person coughs or sneezes near someone. People with symptoms should **stay at home / go to work** and use tissues when they sneeze.
>
> **Gonorrhoea** is passed on via **vectors / sexual intercourse**, so an infected person might try to limit their number of **sexual partners / insect bites** and should always use **condoms / contraceptive pills** if they have intercourse.

B1b Topic 4 — Use, Misuse and Abuse

Infectious Diseases

Q4 The graph shows the change in someone's **body temperature** during a **flu infection**. Their temperature was recorded at the same time every day.

a) What was the maximum body temperature during this illness?

....

b) Approximately how many days after direct contact with someone infected with flu might you start to feel unwell?

....

c) The influenza virus is an example of a microbe spread by horizontal transmission. What does this mean?

....

....

Q5 Pathogens can also be transmitted by **indirect contact**.

a) Complete the table on the right by ticking the correct boxes to match the infectious diseases with their carriers.

The first one has been done for you.

Infectious disease	Vector	Vehicle
sleeping sickness	✓	
typhoid		
malaria		
verrucas		
salmonella		

b) Explain the difference between a vector and a vehicle.

....

c) Give the vector or vehicle that transmits each of the following diseases, and explain how knowing how it is carried can help prevent its spread.

i) Malaria ....

....

ii) Verrucas ....

....

iii) Salmonella ....

....

B1b Topic 4 — Use, Misuse and Abuse

TB — Tuberculosis

Q1 List three typical **symptoms** of active **tuberculosis**.

....

Q2 Tuberculosis is caused by a bacterium called *Mycobacterium tuberculosis*.

How is this bacterium spread from a disease sufferer to a new host? Circle one of the following:

    insect vector   droplet infection   sexual contact   in food / water

Q3 Some groups of people are considered to be at **higher risk** of developing TB than others.

  a) Name **two** of these groups and explain why they are at greater risk than normal.

....

....

....

  b) Describe the action that could be taken by medical professionals to prevent the disease developing in an at-risk individual if they are:

    i) An infant of 3 months. ....

....

    ii) An adult. ....

....

....

Q4 The graph shows the variation in the number of cases of **TB** in the **UK** between 1997 and 2005.

  a) **i)** How many cases were there in 1998?

....

    ii) In which year was the number of cases 6400?

....

  b) Suggest **two** possible reasons why cases of TB have risen in the UK since 1997.

    1. ....

    2. ....

  c) Would you expect the number of cases in a developing country to be lower or higher than in the UK? Give reasons for your answer.

....

....

B1b Topic 4 — Use, Misuse and Abuse

TB — Tuberculosis

Q5 In a lot of cases, people infected with the TB bacterium do **not** immediately develop the disease. Explain the difference between having a **TB infection** and having the **TB disease**.

....

....

Q6 The number of **deaths** due to TB has **decreased** in many **developed countries** since the beginning of the 20th century, particularly since the 1950s.

Tick the boxes to show the factors scientists believe are involved in the decrease in TB fatalities.

- ☐ Improvements in living standards.
- ☐ Compulsory quarantine of anyone thought to be infected.
- ☐ Pasteurisation of milk.
- ☐ Development of a spray used to repel airborne bacteria.
- ☐ Spitting in public places discouraged.

Q7 Patients with TB are given at least three different **antibiotics** at once in order to combat strains with bacterial **resistance**. There are far more **multi-drug** resistant strains of *Mycobacterium tuberculosis* now than there were 50 years ago.

a) Explain how antibiotic-resistant strains of bacteria appear.

....

....

b) Suggest why multi-drug resistant TB bacteria are becoming more common.

....

....

....

Q8 When microbes like TB **mutate** and become **resistant** to an antibiotic, why can't new drugs be produced **quickly**? Give **three** possible reasons.

Think about costs and safety.

1. ....

2. ....

3. ....

Top Tips: You definitely don't want TB. TB's bad. And now there's a new mutated version called Extreme Drug Resistant TB. That's even badder. If you ask me it's a good job we've got pasteurised milk to put on our cereal. And immunisation — that's good too. Not as good as cereal though...

B1b Topic 4 — Use, Misuse and Abuse

Drugs

Q1 Some drugs can only be obtained legally from a **doctor**, others are more **widely available** and some are always **illegal**. Look at the following list of substances.

alcohol, amphetamines, LSD, antibiotics, caffeine, cannabis, paracetamol, cocaine

Put each of these drugs into one of the following three groups:

a) Illegal ....

b) Prescription-only (legal) ....

c) Non-prescription (legal) ....

Q2 Some drugs are **addictive** and can cause **withdrawal symptoms**.

a) What are 'withdrawal symptoms'?

....

b) Name two drugs that can be addictive.

....

Q3 LSD is **less addictive** than cannabis, yet LSD is a **class A** drug and cannabis is **class C**. Suggest why.

....

....

Q4 Drugs can be put into **different groups** according to the effect they have on the **nervous system**.

a) Give one example of a drug that is a:

Stimulant .... Sedative ....

b) Why is it dangerous to drive or operate machinery when under the influence of a sedative?

....

....

c) Caffeine is a legal drug in the UK. Why isn't it dangerous to drive under the influence of this drug?

....

....

Q5 **Alcohol** is a legal drug, although if it is abused over a period of time it can **fatally damage the body**. Describe two **other** risks associated with excessive alcohol intake.

1. ....

2. ....

B1b Topic 4 — Use, Misuse and Abuse

Drugs — Use and Harm

Q1 Look at the following examples of **health problems** and underline any that you think are related to **smoking tobacco**.

Think about the way mumps and cholera are contracted.

strokes mumps bronchitis heart attacks cholera emphysema

Q2 Smoking tobacco can cause many different **health problems**, including cancer. However, the habit is still widespread, mainly because smokers find it **difficult to stop**.

a) Explain why people find it difficult to stop smoking.

....

b) Pregnant women are strongly advised not to smoke. What effect can smoking have on a baby's birth weight?

....

c) Explain how smoking whilst pregnant can cause this problem.

....
....

Q3 The graph shows how the number of **smokers** aged between 35 and 54 in the UK has changed since 1950.

a) Describe the main trends you can see in this graph.

....
....
....
....

b) Why are smokers more likely to suffer from:

i) chest infections ....
....
....

ii) cancers ....
....

B1b Topic 4 — Use, Misuse and Abuse

Drugs — Use and Harm

Q4 In the UK, the legal limit for alcohol in the blood when driving is **80 mg per 100 cm^3**. The table shows the number of 'units' of alcohol in different drinks. One **unit** increases the blood alcohol level by over **20 mg per 100 cm^3** in most people.

DRINK	ALCOHOL UNITS
1 pint of strong lager	3
1 pint of beer	2
1 single measure of whisky	1

a) Bill drinks two pints of strong lager. How many units of alcohol has he had? ....

b) Is Bill's blood alcohol level likely to mean that he cannot legally drive? Explain your answer.

....

....

Assume he drank the pints fairly quickly.

c) Explain why it can be dangerous to drive a car after drinking alcohol.

....

Q5 As well as **altered behaviour** leading to accidents and poor decisions, alcohol can have **damaging physical effects** if it is abused.

a) Alcohol can cause **dehydration**. What effect does this have on the brain?

....

b) Which other organ is often damaged by excessive alcohol intake? ....

Q6 **Solvents** are useful substances that are sometimes **misused**.

a) Give **three** examples of useful substances that contain potentially dangerous solvents.

....

b) Use some of the words in the box to fill in the gaps and complete the passage.

| stimulants | breathing | depressants | lungs | decreasing | brain damage | eyes | memory |

Solvents, like alcohol, are in a group of drugs called ....

Drugs like these affect the nervous system by .... the speed at which

nerve impulses are passed across synapses. Long-term solvent abuse often causes

.... — symptoms of which include personality changes, trouble

sleeping or loss of .... Solvents also damage the ....

and can cause .... difficulties. Solvents can even kill, and this can

happen the very first time you use them.

Top Tips: Tobacco, alcohol and solvents are all totally **legal** substances, but they're all potentially dangerous drugs too. Solvents are dangerous if they are **misused**, alcohol is dangerous if used to **excess**, and cigarettes are, well, just full of nasty poisonous chemicals.

B1b Topic 4 — Use, Misuse and Abuse

Painkillers

Q1 **Paracetamol** is an over-the-counter drug — you **don't** need a prescription from a doctor to obtain it.

a) Name two specific symptoms that are relieved by paracetamol.

....

b) Suggest two reasons why is it important to always read the label before taking even over-the-counter drugs like paracetamol.

....

....

c) Paracetamol is a fairly safe drug, but can be very dangerous if too much is taken at once. Explain fully why this is.

....

....

....

Q2 **Opiates** are a group of drugs which all have **pain-relieving properties**.

a) Which of the following drugs are opiates? Tick the boxes next to the correct answers.

- ☐ cannabinoids   ☐ opium
- ☐ ibuprofen   ☐ morphine
- ☐ paracetamol   ☐ aspirin
- ☐ codeine   ☐ amphetamines

b) What are all of the opiate drugs derived from?

....

c) Why are some opiates only ever given to patients who are under the supervision of a doctor?

....

....

Top Tips: Opium's been used for thousands of years, and it turns out that some of the most famous authors of all time used it. Huxley, Coleridge, Crabbe... Some of them used it really regularly too. Although trying it in your English exams would definitely be a pretty bad move...

B1b Topic 4 — Use, Misuse and Abuse

Painkillers

Q3 **Cannabis** is an **illegal** drug, but some people still use it to relieve the pain caused by **chronic diseases**.

Remember, 'chronic' means long-lasting, not just really bad.

a) What are cannabinoids?

....

b) Give two examples of chronic diseases for which there is anecdotal evidence in favour of cannabis as a useful painkiller.

....

Q4 The benefits of some drugs, such as the painkilling chemicals found in **cannabis**, have not been investigated very thoroughly — evidence of the benefits is mainly **anecdotal**.

a) Explain what is meant by the term anecdotal evidence.

....

b) Why has there been so little research into the medical uses of cannabis compounds?

....

....

c) One breakthrough in the 1980s seemed to support the anecdotal evidence. Explain what this was.

....

Q5 Different **painkillers** work in different ways.

a) i) Explain fully how aspirin relieves mild pain and reduces swelling.

....

....

....

ii) Give an example of another painkiller which works in a similar way.

....

b) i) Explain fully how morphine works as a strong painkiller.

....

....

ii) Give an example of another painkiller that works in a similar way.

....

B1b Topic 4 — Use, Misuse and Abuse

Mixed Questions — B1b Topics 3 & 4

Q1 **Reflex actions** are **automatic responses** to a stimulus.

a) Give one advantage of reflex actions to the body.

....

b) Which part of the nervous system is used to coordinate a reflex response?

....

c) Below are three situations which would cause reflex actions.

A: Stepping on a drawing pin with bare feet.   **B:** A bright light shining in the eyes.

C: Smelling food when hungry.

Saliva production often increases when you smell food.

Complete the table below for each of the examples given above.

	A	B	C
stimulus			
receptor			
effector			
response			

d) In what part of the brain is information from the eyes processed?

....

Q2 **Hormones** are **chemical messengers** that affect particular target cells in the body.

a) Choose the hormone or hormones from the list in blue to go with each of the statements below.

   FSH   oestrogen   insulin   progesterone

   i) Involved in the menstrual cycle. ....

   ii) Produced in the pancreas. ....

   iii) Stimulates the ovaries to produce oestrogen. ....

   iv) There are receptors for this in the liver. ....

   v) Contained in the combined contraceptive pill. ....

b) Hormones can affect different parts of the body at the same time. Explain how.

....

....

c) When diabetics inject insulin, do their blood sugar levels increase or decrease?

....

B1b Topic 4 — Use, Misuse and Abuse

Mixed Questions — B1b Topics 3 & 4

Q3 Tuberculosis (TB) is a disease spread by droplet infection.

a) Circle the correct word from each pair to complete the sentences below.

The microorganism that causes TB is transmitted by droplet infection / a vector.
This is an example of vertical / horizontal transmission.

b) Explain how the body's defence systems would try to prevent the TB bacterium entering the lungs.

....

c) Name the vaccine that can be used to prevent TB. ....

d) Explain why the treatment for TB involves three or four antibiotics, rather than just one.

....

Q4 The blood is a huge transport system.

a) i) Give the name of the blood cell shown on the right.

....

ii) What is the function of this cell?

....

b) The cell on the right transports oxygen to all parts of the body.

Give two ways in which this cell is adapted to perform its job.
Briefly explain how each adaptation allows it to do its job well.

....

....

....

c) Microorganisms such as HIV can pass from a mother's blood to her child's through the placenta.

Is this horizontal or vertical transmission? ....

Q5 Drugs interfere with the chemical reactions occurring in your body.

Michael wakes up the morning after his birthday party. He has a terrible headache.

a) Michael's symptoms were caused by drinking too much alcohol at his party.
Explain why too much alcohol has this effect.

....

b) Michael decides to take double the normal dose of paracetamol to
ease the pain of his headache. Explain why this is **not** a good idea.

....

....

B1b Topic 4 — Use, Misuse and Abuse

Respiration

Q1 Part of the **word equation** for one type of **respiration** is shown below.

  a) Complete the equation for respiration.

  .... + oxygen → carbon dioxide + ... + ...

  b) What type of respiration is this? ....

Q2 Which of these statements is **not** true of respiration? Underline the correct answer.

  It takes place in every cell of your body.   It releases energy from food.

  It is another word for breathing.   It can be aerobic or anaerobic.

Q3 Give three things that the body uses the **energy** obtained in respiration for.

  ....

  ....

Q4 Draw lines to match the **body part** or **process** to the correct description.

  capillaries — The system that provides the food source needed for respiration.

  circulatory system — The gradual movement of particles from areas of higher concentration to areas of lower concentration.

  diffusion — The smallest blood vessels that carry blood to all body cells.

  digestive system — The system that carries substances like glucose, oxygen and carbon dioxide around your body.

Q5 The diagram shows **blood** passing through **muscle tissue**.

  a) On the diagram, draw labelled arrows to show whether **oxygen (O_2)**, **glucose (G)** and **carbon dioxide (CO_2)** move **into** or **out of** the muscle cells.

  b) Explain how these substances move into and out of the blood in terms of concentration gradients.

  ....

  ....

  ....

  ....

Respiration and Exercise

Q1 Jim is a keen runner. He takes part in a 400 metre race. The **graph** below shows Jim's **breathing rate** before, during and after the race.

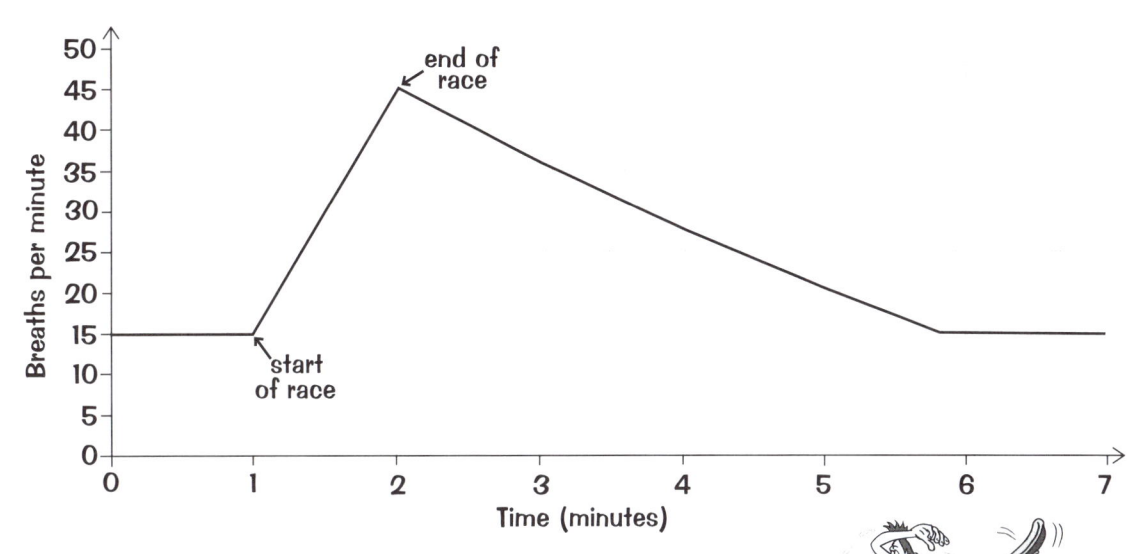

a) How much does Jim's breathing rate go up during the race?

.... **breaths per minute**

b) Explain why exercise makes Jim's breathing rate increase.

....

....

....

c) Why **doesn't** Jim's breathing rate return to normal immediately after the race?

Think about the products of anaerobic respiration.

....

....

....

Q2 Amy used a **digital monitor** to measure how her body changed during exercise.

a) What three things could Amy monitor?

....

b) The monitor allowed Amy to continuously record the changes that happened to her body. Give two other advantages of using digital monitors.

....

....

B2 Topic 1 — Inside Living Cells

Respiration and Exercise

Q3 Humans can respire **aerobically** — if there isn't enough oxygen available we can also respire **anaerobically**.

a) Give **two** advantages of aerobic respiration over anaerobic respiration.

1. ....

....

2. ....

....

b) In what circumstances would a human start respiring anaerobically?

....

....

c) Mary-Kate doesn't like sport and is unfit. Ashley is sporty and on the county hockey team. Both girls run an 800 m race. Which girl will start respiring **anaerobically** first?

....

d) Write the **word equation** for anaerobic respiration in humans.

.... → .... + ...

Q4 Roy wants to find out which of his friends has the shortest **'recovery' time**. Your recovery time is how long it takes for your pulse rate to **return to normal** after exercise. Roy tests each of his friends separately. He measures their **pulse rate**, then asks them to **run** for 2 minutes. After they've finished running, he measures their pulse rate at 15 second intervals until it has returned to normal.

a) Write down **two** things Roy should do to ensure it is a **fair test**.

Think about keeping things constant.

1. ....

....

2. ....

....

b) Here is a sketch of Roy's results. Which of his friends had the **shortest** recovery time?

....

KEY
— Jim
— Saeed
— Bonnie

B2 Topic 1 — Inside Living Cells

Evaluating Health Claims

Q1 Two reports on **low-fat foods** were published on one day. **Report A** appeared in a tabloid paper. It said that the manufacturers of 'Chewy Bites' have shown that the latest girl band, Kandyfloss, lost weight using their product. **Report B** appeared in the *Journal of Medicine* and reported how 6000 volunteers lost weight during a trial of an experimental drug.

Which of these reports is likely to be the most reliable and why?

....

....

....

Q2 Three **weight loss methods** appeared in the headlines last week.

① **Hollywood star swears carrot soup aids weight loss**

② **Survey of 10 000 dieters shows it's exercise that counts**

③ **Atkins works! 5000 in study lose weight... but what about their health?**

a) Which of these headlines are more likely to refer to **scientific studies**? Explain your answer.

....

....

b) Why might following the latest celebrity diet not always help you lose weight?

....

....

Q3 **Statins** are drugs that lower the levels of 'bad' cholesterol in the blood. A drug trial to test their effectiveness involved 6000 patients with **high cholesterol levels**. 3000 patients were given statins and 3000 were not. Both groups were advised to make lifestyle changes to lower their cholesterol. The decrease in their cholesterol levels compared to their levels at the start is shown on the graph.

a) Why was the group without statins included?

....

b) Suggest a conclusion that can be drawn from these results.

....

....

B2 Topic 1 — Inside Living Cells

Evaluating Health Claims

Q4 The **UK government** has a responsibility to educate the public about how to have a **healthy diet**.

FOOD	MORE	LESS
Fruit		
Salt		
Sugars		
Oily fish		
Vegetables		
Fat		

a) The advice the government provides suggests that most people need to cut their intake of some foods and to try to eat more of others.

Tick the boxes in the table on the right to show how you think the average person in the UK should adjust their diet to conform to government advice.

b) Name **two** organisations that provide the government with evidence to support the advice that they give.

1. ....

2. ....

Q5 After Amanda's father died of **heart disease**, she decided to record the amount of **exercise** she did, to see if it was enough to reduce her risk of heart disease. On the right is her exercise diary for one week.

DAY	ACTIVITY
Sunday	Run with the dog, 10 minutes.
Monday	Run with the dog, 10 minutes.
Tuesday	Run with the dog, 10 minutes. Swim 20 minutes.
Wednesday	Run with the dog, 10 minutes.
Thursday	Run with the dog, 10 minutes.
Friday	Run with the dog, 10 minutes. Swim 20 minutes.
Saturday	Run with the dog, 10 minutes.

a) What is the total time Amanda spent exercising last week?

....

b) What is the current UK government recommendation for the amount of exercise a person should do each week? Give your answer in **minutes per week**.

....

c) What is the difference between this total and Amanda's total?

....

d) Until quite recently, the amount of exercise recommended by the government was lower than the current recommendation. Explain why the advice changed.

....

....

....

Top Tips: The overall message here is **don't believe everything you read**. You have to carry out proper trials, with a large sample size, scientists who know what they're doing, and a method that ensures a fair comparison, before you can begin to suggest that something is good or bad for you.

B2 Topic 1 — Inside Living Cells

25.4.10

DNA — Making Proteins

Q1 The following questions are about **DNA**.

a) What is the function of DNA?
   gives instructions to make proteins

b) What name is given to the shape of a DNA molecule? *Double helix*

c) How many different bases make up the DNA structure? *4*

d) Which bases pair up together?
   Adenine — thymine, Guanine — cytosine

Q2 Tick the boxes to show whether the following statements are **true** or **false**.

		True	False
a)	Genes are sections of DNA that code for specific proteins.	✓	
b)	Each amino acid is coded for by a set of four base pairs.		✓
c)	Each cell contains different genes, which is why we have different types of cell.		✓
d)	Proteins are made by ribosomes.	✓	
e)	RNA is a messenger molecule that communicates between DNA and the ribosomes.	✓	
f)	RNA contains two strands, like DNA.		✓

Q3 Answer the following questions to explain how a section of code on a **DNA molecule** can be used to build a new **protein**.

a) How is a molecule of messenger RNA formed from a molecule of DNA?
   The two DNA strands unzip. A molecule of RNA is made using the DNA as a template. Base

b) How do RNA and ribosomes work together to build proteins?
   ....
   ....

Q4 On the section of **DNA** shown:

A G G C T A G C C A A T C G C C G A A G C T C A
T C C G A T C G G T T A G C G

a) Complete the lower sequence of bases.

b) Calculate how many amino acids are coded for by this section of DNA.
   ....

B2 Topic 1 — Inside Living Cells

Using Microorganisms

Q1 Circle the correct word in each pair to complete the sentences below.

Microorganisms use **photosynthesis** / **respiration** to release **energy** / **oxygen** from **sugars** / **salts**. If this process is anaerobic it is also known as **distillation** / **fermentation**.

Q2 Some microorganisms can respire **aerobically** or **anaerobically**.

a) What is the difference between aerobic and anaerobic respiration?
....

b) How is aerobic respiration used in the process of breadmaking?
....
....

Q3 Number the following stages in the process of **making cheese** to put them into the correct order.

.... An increased acidity of the milk causes curdling.

.... Lactose is converted into lactic acid by the bacteria.

.... The curdles are compressed into cheese.

.... Bacteria are placed into milk.

.... The milk becomes more acidic.

.... The bacteria feed on the milk, which contains a sugar called lactose.

Q4 Sarah has been diagnosed with **type 1 diabetes**. She has been told that she needs to have daily injections of a **hormone**.

a) What is the name of this hormone? ....

b) Give **two** reasons why it's better for diabetics to use hormones produced by microorganisms than hormones from animals such as pigs.

1. ....

2. ....

Top Tips: Bacteria aren't the only things that can respire anaerobically — if you hold both arms out from your sides for as long as you can, your shoulders start to burn. That's because your muscles start respiring anaerobically, producing lactic acid, which causes the pain... Nice.

B2 Topic 1 — Inside Living Cells

Using Microorganisms

Q5 The diagram below shows a **fermenter** that can be used for producing **mycoprotein**.

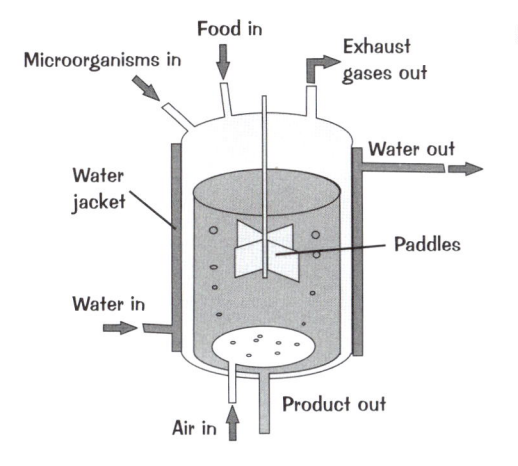

a) Explain the purpose of each of the following:

i) the water jacket

....

ii) the air supply

....

iii) the paddles

....

b) Before fermentation begins, the fermenter is usually filled with steam and then cooled. Why is this done?

....

c) What is mycoprotein used for?

....

Q6 a) Match the descriptions below to the different stages of insulin production by putting the correct letter next to the diagram.

A The hormone produced by the bacteria is purified and can then be used as a treatment.

B The bacteria are cultivated until millions of identical bacteria have grown.

C Another enzyme cuts the bacterial DNA so that the human section of DNA can be inserted.

D A human DNA sample is taken.

E Enzymes are used to cut the human insulin gene from the human DNA.

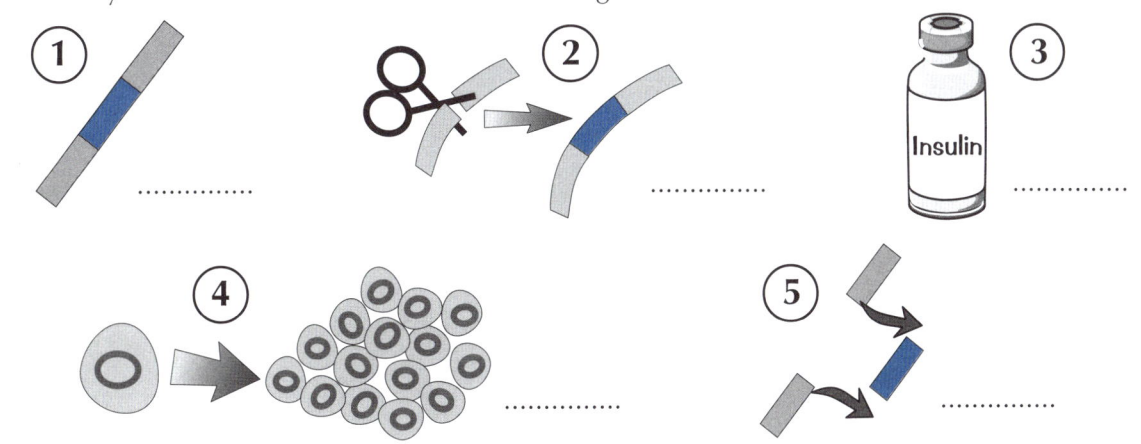

b) Arrange the numbers to give the steps in the correct order.

....

B2 Topic 1 — Inside Living Cells

Using Microorganisms

Q7 Circle the correct word in each pair to complete the passage below.

Some bacteria / viruses that cause disease can be killed or stopped from growing by hormones / antibiotics. These are produced by other microorganisms — for example, insulin / penicillin is produced by a virus / mould. This mould can be grown in a fermenter using a liquid / solid culture medium that contains starch / sugars and nitrates / sodium.

Q8 Give three advantages of producing foods using microorganisms rather than other organisms.

1. ....
2. ....
3. ....

Q9 A group of students set up the experiment below to simulate the conditions in a fermenter.

1. Make up the culture medium and put it into a sterile flask.
2. Add a sample of the microorganism (yeast).
3. Seal the flask with a ventilated bung that lets gas out but not in.
4. Mix thoroughly then place in the incubator at 37 °C.
5. Remove from the incubator for mixing every 15 minutes.

a) Name three substances that a culture medium would usually contain.

....

b) George set up his experiment but forgot to put the flask into the incubator. What effect would this have on his experiment?

....

c) Give one reason why the contents of the flask needed to be mixed regularly.

....

d) The teacher asked pupils to take a small sample of their culture medium and test it with Universal Indicator paper. Why did they need to do this?

....

e) Do you think that the yeast cells were respiring aerobically or anaerobically? Explain your answer.

....

B2 Topic 1 — Inside Living Cells

B2 Topic 2 — Divide and Develop

Growth in Organisms

Q1 If an organism increases in size or weight, it is **growing**.

a) Give one way to measure the **size** of an organism.

....

b) How do you measure the **dry weight** of an organism?

....

Q2 A Year 10 class investigated the **heights** of the class members. The results are shown on the graph.

a) What type of variation did they investigate? Circle your choice.

    Continuous / **Discontinuous**

b) What was the **shortest** height in the group?

....

c) What was the **tallest** height in the group?

....

d) Into what range of heights did most pupils fall? Circle your choice.

    141–150 cm   151–160 cm   161–170 cm

e) Give three things that influence height in humans.

1. .... 2. .... 3. ....

Q3 Some animals can **regenerate** parts of their bodies.

a) What does 'regenerate' mean?

....

b) Give an example of regeneration.

....

Q4 **Growth factors** are naturally produced in the bodies of animals.

a) What are growth factors?

....

b) Why is it illegal for athletes to take growth factor drugs?

....

c) Give **two** possible side effects of using growth factor drugs.

....

Cell Division — Mitosis

Q1 Decide whether the following statements are **true** or **false**.

		True	False
a)	Human body cells are diploid.	☐	☐
b)	There are 20 pairs of chromosomes in a human cheek cell.	☐	☐
c)	Chromosomes are found in the cytoplasm of a cell.	☐	☐
d)	Before a cell divides by mitosis, it duplicates its DNA.	☐	☐
e)	Mitosis is where a cell splits to create two genetically identical copies.	☐	☐
f)	Each new cell produced in mitosis gets one chromosome from each pair.	☐	☐
g)	Organisms use mitosis in order to grow.	☐	☐
h)	Organisms do not use mitosis to replace damaged cells.	☐	☐

Q2 The following diagram shows the different stages of **mitosis**. Write a short description to explain each stage.

a) ....

b) ....

c) ....
....

d) ....
....

e) ....

Q3 Write a definition of the **Hayflick limit** for a science dictionary. Include in your definition the Hayflick limit for most **human cells** and examples of two cell types that have **no** Hayflick limit.

....
....
....

B2 Topic 2 — Divide and Develop

Cell Division — Meiosis

Q1 Circle the correct word from each pair to complete the sentences below.

a) Gametes are sex cells. During **asexual / sexual** reproduction two gametes combine to form a new cell that will grow into a new organism.

b) Gametes are **diploid / haploid**. This means they have **one copy / two copies** of each chromosome. This is so that when two gametes combine the resulting cell has the right number of chromosomes.

c) Human body cells have **23 / 46** chromosomes and human gametes have **23 / 46** chromosomes. When the gametes combine you get **23 / 46** chromosomes again.

Q2 Tick the boxes to show if each statement is true of **mitosis**, **meiosis** or **both**.

		Mitosis	Meiosis
a)	Gives new cells that each have half the original number of chromosomes.	☐	☐
b)	The chromosomes line up in the centre of the cell.	☐	☐
c)	Forms cells that are genetically identical.	☐	☐
d)	In humans, this only happens in the reproductive organs.	☐	☐

Q3 Draw lines to match each description of the stage of **meiosis** to the right diagram below.

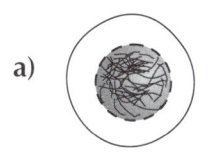

a) — The pairs are pulled apart, mixing up the mother and father's chromosomes into the new cells. This creates genetic variation.

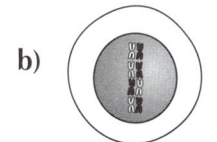

b) — Before the cell starts to divide it duplicates its DNA to produce an exact copy.

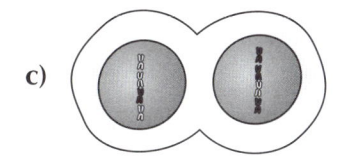

c) — There are now 4 gametes, each containing half the original number of chromosomes.

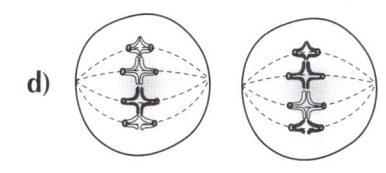

d) — For the first meiotic division the chromosomes line up in their pairs across the centre of the cell.

e) — The chromosomes line up across the centre of the nucleus ready for the second division, and the two arms of each chromosome are pulled apart.

Top Tips: It's easy to get confused between **mitosis** and **meiosis**. Mitosis produces cells for growth and replaces damaged cells. Meiosis is for sexual reproduction and creates gametes.

B2 Topic 2 — Divide and Develop

Stem Cells and Differentiation

Q1 Tick the correct boxes to show whether the following statements are **true** or **false**.   True   False

a) Cells in an early embryo are unspecialised. ☐ ☐

b) Blood cells are undifferentiated. ☐ ☐

c) Nerve cells are specialised cells. ☐ ☐

d) Adult stem cells are as versatile as embryonic stem cells. ☐ ☐

e) Stem cells in bone marrow can differentiate into any type of cell. ☐ ☐

Q2 Scientists in the UK are carrying out research into the use of stem cells in **medicine**.

a) Describe one way in which stem cells are **already** used in medicine.

....

b) Describe how it might be possible to use embryonic stem cells to treat disease in the future.

....

....

Q3 People have **different opinions** when it comes to embryonic **stem cell research**.

a) Give one argument **in favour** of stem cell research. ....

....

b) Give one argument **against** stem cell research. ....

....

Q4 It is illegal to **terminate pregnancies** in the UK after the foetus is a certain age.

a) What is this age in weeks? ....

b) Explain why the limit was set at this particular stage of pregnancy.

....

....

c) Give two situations in which an abortion may be allowed after this limit has passed.

....

....

d) Explain why some people feel that abortion is unethical.

....

....

B2 Topic 2 — Divide and Develop

Growth in Plants

Q1 Green plants were grown in a lab to investigate the effect of **mineral deficiency** on plant growth.

a) Plant A had yellow leaves. Which mineral was in short supply? ....

b) Plant B was grown in a solution low in nitrates. What effect would this have?

....

c) Why would a plant grown in a solution low in phosphates have poor growth?

....

Q2 Michelle put her baby's paddling pool on the lawn. The sunny weather made the grass around the pool **grow quickly**, but when Michelle moved the pool she found that the grass under it had **died**. Explain why.

....

....

Q3 Nick had heard that plants grow better when they are **warm**. He put his favourite plant on top of a hot radiator and kept it well watered, but the plant **died**.

a) Why do plants grow better when they are warm?

....

b) Explain why Nick's plant died.

....

....

Q4 Why do plants need:

a) Carbon dioxide? ....

b) Oxygen? ....

Q5 Rory carried out an investigation into the **distribution** of marram grass in an area between the shoreline and dense forest. His results are shown in the graph below.

a) Describe the distribution of marram grass.

....

....

b) Suggest a reason for this distribution.

....

....

B2 Topic 2 — Divide and Develop

Growth in Plants: Plant Hormones

Q1 Three **plant shoots** were set up with a **light stimulus**. The diagram shows the shape of each shoot before and after.

a) Which part of the plant shoot is most sensitive to light?

....

b) Which plant hormone controls the growth of the tip?

....

c) On each picture, shade in the region that contains the most of this hormone.

Q2 Growth hormones can change the **direction** in which shoots and roots grow.

a) Complete the diagrams below to show which way the root or shoot **will grow** and explain your answer with reference to growth hormones.

i) [ROOT diagram] Explanation: ....

ii) [SHOOT diagram] Explanation: ....

iii) [ROOT with water diagram] Explanation: ....

b) Explain why these different responses are important in the survival of the seedling.

....

Q3 Erica bought a **seedless satsuma** to school and asked her teacher why it contained no seeds.

a) How do fruits (with seeds) normally develop?

....

b) Explain how seedless citrus fruits are grown.

....

B2 Topic 2 — Divide and Develop

Selective Breeding

Q1 Circle the correct word(s) in each pair to complete the passage below.

> Selective breeding leads to less **variety** / DNA in the gene pool of a population.
>
> All of the organisms in the population will be sterile / **closely related**.
>
> This means that they will have **similar** / different characteristics.
>
> That can be an advantage, e.g. if they all have high temperatures / **milk yields**.
>
> However, it can also be a disadvantage, e.g. if they are all resistant / **susceptible**
>
> to the same disease.

Q2 Garfield wants to breed one type of plant for its **fruit**, and another as an **ornamental house plant**.

  a) Suggest **two** characteristics that he should select for in each kind of plant.

  Fruit plant: 1. ....
  2. ....

  Ornamental house plant: 1. ....
  2. ....

  b) Why is selective breeding also called 'artificial' selection?

  ....
  ....

Q3 Some breeds of **sheep** have been bred for their high level of **fertility**.

  a) Describe how selective breeding from a sheep stock with **low fertility** could produce a breed that has a **higher number of offspring**.

  ....
  ....

  b) Explain why some farmed sheep breeds are likely to suffer from genetic disorders.

  .... *Many genetic disorders are recessive, i.e. you have to have two copies of the same faulty allele before you develop the condition.*
  ....
  ....
  ....

B2 Topic 2 — Divide and Develop

Selective Breeding

Q4 The graph shows the **milk yield** for a population of cows over three generations.

a) Do you think that selective breeding is likely to have been used with these cows? Explain your answer.

....

....

b) What is the increase in the average milk yield per cow from generation 1 to generation 2?

....

c) What is the smallest milk yield recorded for generation 3?

....

d) Suggest why the milk yield will reach a maximum limit after many generations.

....

Q5 The red **jungle fowl** is thought to be the wild ancestor of all farm-bred chickens. Farm-bred chickens have been produced by **selective breeding** for egg laying.

a) Suggest three ways in which farm-bred chickens are likely to differ from wild red jungle fowls.

....

....

b) Suggest how selective breeding in chickens might harm the welfare of the birds.

....

....

Q6 There are two varieties of **wheat plants** that have the characteristics outlined below:

WHEAT PLANT	GRAIN YIELD	RESISTANCE TO BAD WEATHER
Tall plant	High	Low
Dwarf plant	Low	High

How could a wheat plant be created with a **high yield** and **high resistance** to bad weather?

....

....

B2 Topic 2 — Divide and Develop

Cloning and Genetic Modification

Q1 **Dolly the sheep** was born in 1996.

a) Explain why the birth of this lamb was so significant from a scientific point of view.

....

b) Describe the process that was used to create Dolly the sheep.

....

....

....

Q2 In nature, cloning involves a single parent, but the procedure used to create Dolly the sheep involved **three 'parents'** as outlined in the table below.

Parent	Involvement in creating Dolly
1	Provided the egg cell
2	Provided the diploid nucleus
3	Embryo implanted into the uterus

Dolly was genetically identical to only one of her three 'parents'. Which parent was this? Explain your answer.

....

....

Q3 Describe the **disadvantages** of cloning, in relation to:

a) Success rate ....

....

b) Genetic defects ....

....

c) The immune system ....

....

Top Tips: Poor Dolly had to be put down (aged six) due to lung disease — that's only **half** the age sheep of her breed can reach. They're not sure if it was due to her being a **clone**, but it's certainly true that clones tend to suffer **health problems**.

B2 Topic 2 — Divide and Develop

Cloning and Genetic Modification

Q4 Answer the following questions about **genetic modification**.

a) What does genetic modification mean?

....

....

b) At which point in its life cycle should an organism be genetically modified?

....

c) Explain how genetic modification could be of use in treating genetic disorders.

....

....

Q5 Explain why some people are **concerned** about genetic modification.

....

....

....

Q6 **Pyrethrum** is an **insecticide**. It is found naturally in chrysanthemum plants.

a) A gene to make pyrethrum could be used to improve the pest resistance of soya plants. Put these stages in order to show how this could be done:

A	Soya plants display pest resistance.
B	Identify the pyrethrum gene.
C	Insert the gene into the DNA of a soya plant.
D	Extract the gene from the chrysanthemum DNA.

Order: ...., ..., ..., ...

b) Give one advantage and one disadvantage of producing GM soya in this way.

....

....

....

B2 Topic 2 — Divide and Develop

Gene Therapy

Q1 Genes code for **proteins** in the body. Inherited disorders are the result of inheriting a **faulty copy** of a gene.

a) What happens to the protein if the gene is faulty?

....

b) Give the name of a disease or disorder caused by:

i) A single faulty gene. ....

ii) A combination of inherited genes and environmental factors. ....

Q2 It is hoped that **gene therapy** may be useful in treating genetic disorders.

a) What is gene therapy?

....

....

b) Outline the problems associated with gene therapy.

....

....

Q3 Decide whether each of the following statements is **true** or **false**.   True False

a) Gene therapy involves inserting functional versions of faulty proteins into cells. ☐ ☐

b) Suicide genes are used to attack the cells that cause cystic fibrosis. ☐ ☐

c) Some scientists worry that suicide genes could be taken up by healthy cells. ☐ ☐

d) In the UK, embryos at risk of inheriting diseases are genetically modified. ☐ ☐

e) Gene therapy would prevent diseases being passed on to the next generation. ☐ ☐

Q4 It is hoped that gene therapy could one day be used to treat **cancer**.

Outline one possible method that could be used to treat cancer with gene therapy.

....

....

....

B2 Topic 2 — Divide and Develop

Mixed Questions — B2 Topics 1 & 2

Q1 The **Large White** is a breed of pig that is farmed for meat. Large Whites can tolerate harsh weather, and the females are good mothers that produce a lot of offspring. **Selective breeding** from wild pigs has produced the Large White.

a) Choose one of the features of the Large White and suggest how this is an advantage in farming.

....

b) Explain how the characteristics above would have been produced through selective breeding.

....

....

c) If a **gene** that caused Large Whites to produce particularly large litters of offspring was isolated, how might this be used to improve the litter sizes of another species?

....

....

d) A farmer breeds a pig that lives for an unexpectedly long time. It remains healthy and produces many more litters during its lifetime than the average pig. He decides to clone it to reproduce these useful features exactly. Explain why this may not have the desired effect.

....

....

Q2 Several students **germinated beans**. When the beans had germinated, they turned them sideways so that the roots and shoots were **horizontal**. The results after three days are shown below.

a) Name the hormones responsible for these changes.

....

b) Explain the results observed.

....

....

c) Give **three** other factors that affect the **growth** and **distribution** of plants.

1. ....

2. ....

3. ....

B2 Topic 2 — Divide and Develop

Mixed Questions — B2 Topics 1 & 2

Q3 Humans can respire **aerobically** and **anaerobically**.

a) Give a definition of respiration, including where it happens in the body.

....

b) Complete the following sentences about anaerobic respiration in humans.

> Anaerobic respiration is respiration without ....
>
> A waste product, ... , is produced. ....
>
> energy is released during anaerobic respiration than during aerobic respiration.

c) Anaerobic respiration is not as efficient as aerobic respiration. Why is it still useful to us?

....

....

d) Some **bacteria** can respire anaerobically.
Explain how certain anaerobic bacteria can be useful in cheese making.

....

....

Q4 Two studies into the **Atkins diet** were published in the New England Journal of Medicine in 2003. The first tested 132 obese patients, and the second tested 63 patients. Both concluded that patients on the Atkins diet lost slightly **more** weight than patients on a conventional low-fat diet.

a) Give three reasons why this is likely to be a trustworthy conclusion.

1. ....

2. ....

3. ....

b) Both these studies noted that longer and larger studies were still needed to determine the long-term safety of the Atkins diet.

Explain why the UK government does **not** recommend Atkins as part of a healthy diet.

....

....

Q5 **Useful genes** can be transferred into plants and animals at an early stage in their development. Outline **one** use of this technique.

....

....

B2 Topic 2 — Divide and Develop

Mixed Questions — B2 Topics 1 & 2

Q6 One way that organisms **grow** is by making new cells by **mitosis**.

The graph shows how the amount of DNA per cell changes as a cell undergoes two cell divisions by mitosis. Point C on the graph is the time when the chromosomes first become visible in the new cells.

a) Describe and explain what is happening to the DNA during stage A.

....

....

b) Describe another change happening in the cell during this stage.

....

c) What happens at time B?

....

Q7 In the future **gene therapy** could be used to treat genetic disorders such as **cystic fibrosis** (CF). John is CF sufferer. He and his wife Mary are planning to start a family.

a) If John could be successfully treated with gene therapy for cystic fibrosis, why would his children still be at risk of inheriting the faulty version of the gene?

....

....

....

b) If Mary was a carrier, how could John and Mary be sure of having a child without the faulty CF gene?

....

....

Q8 Young spiders that lose a leg can **grow** another one — this type of growth is called **regeneration**.

a) Young spiders contain a lot of **stem cells**. Explain why stem cells are needed for regeneration.

....

b) Adult spiders are **not** able to regenerate lost body parts. Suggest a reason for this.

....

B2 Topic 2 — Divide and Develop

Mixed Questions — B2 Topics 1 & 2

Q9 Mosquitoes have **three pairs** of **chromosomes** in their body cells. The diagram shows a cell from a mosquito which is about to divide by **meiosis**.

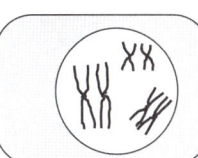

a) Below, draw the chromosomes in one of the cells produced from this cell:

i) after the first division stage of meiosis.

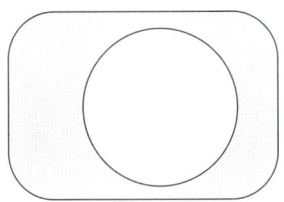

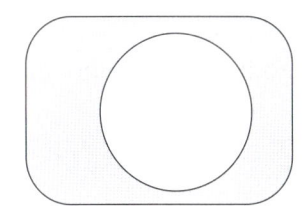

ii) after the second division stage of meiosis.

b) Describe what happens to the chromosomes at the following stages:

i) the first meiotic division. ....

....

ii) the second meiotic division. ....

....

Q10 **Proteins** are large molecules coded for by **DNA**.

a) Explain how each of the following are involved in building **new proteins**.

i) Genes ....

ii) Free amino acids ....

iii) Base triplets ....

iv) RNA ....

v) Ribosomes ....

b) Some **human diseases** are caused by a **lack** of a **working protein**, e.g. people with type 1 diabetes don't produce enough of the protein insulin or don't produce any at all.
Describe how microorganisms are used to treat diabetes.

....

....

....

Q11 Circle the correct word from each pair to complete the passage below.

The climate in some countries makes it hard to farm animals. Because animals are an important source of protein / fibre, an alternative is needed. Mycoprotein / Penicillin is one possibility. This is obtained from a bacteria / fungus that respires anaerobically / aerobically. Microorganisms grow more slowly / quickly than animals, they are easy to look after, and some can use waste / heat as a source of food.

B2 Topic 2 — Divide and Develop

Plants and Photosynthesis

Q1 Plant and animal cells have **similarities** and **differences**.
Complete each statement below by circling the correct words.

a) Plant / Animal cells, but not plant / animal cells, contain chloroplasts.

b) Plant cells have vacuoles / cytoplasm containing cell sap.

c) Both plant and animal cells / Only plant cells / Only animal cells have cell membranes.

d) Chloroplasts are where respiration / photosynthesis occurs, which makes glucose / water.

Q2 This question is about the **content** and **function** of cellular structures.

a) State what each of the following cell structures contains or is made of.

  i) The **nucleus** contains ....

  ii) **Chloroplasts** contain ....

  iii) The **cell wall** is made of ....

b) Explain the function of these cellular structures.

  i) The **nucleus** ....

  ii) **Chloroplasts** ....

  iii) The **cell wall** ....

Q3 **Photosynthesis** is the process that produces 'food' in plants.
Use some of the words below to complete the equation for photosynthesis.

oxygen   carbon dioxide   nitrogen   water   glucose   sodium chloride

.... + ... $\xrightarrow[\text{chlorophyll}]{\text{sunlight}}$ .... + ...

Q4 Decide whether each of the following statements is **true** or **false**.   True   False

a) Photosynthesis happens inside the chloroplasts.   ☐ ☐

b) Photosynthesis happens in all plant cells.   ☐ ☐

c) Plants absorb carbon dioxide from the air.   ☐ ☐

d) Plant cells don't respire.   ☐ ☐

e) Sunlight provides the energy for photosynthesis.   ☐ ☐

Q5 Humans use a lot of plants as **food**, but also use materials produced by plants in other ways. Give three ways in which **plant materials** are used (apart from as food) and include an **example** of each.

....

....

....

B2 Topic 3 — Energy Flow

Rate of Photosynthesis

Q1 Define the term **'limiting factor'**.

....

Q2 Seth investigated the effect of different concentrations of **carbon dioxide** on the rate of photosynthesis of his Swiss cheese plant. The results are shown on the graph below.

a) Describe the effect on the rate of photosynthesis of increasing the concentration of CO_2.

....

....

....

b) Explain why all the lines level off eventually.

....

Think about other limiting factors.

....

Q3 **Average summer temperatures** in different habitats around the world are recorded in the table below.

Habitat	Temperature (°C)
Forest	19
Arctic	0
Desert	32
Grassland	22
Rainforest	27

a) Plot a **bar chart** for these results on the grid.

b) From the values for temperature, in which area would you expect the fewest plants to grow?

....

c) Suggest a reason for your answer above using the terms **enzymes** and **photosynthesis**.

....

....

d) Explain why very few plants can grow in the desert even though it has a much higher average temperature than the rainforest where many varieties of plants can grow.

....

....

B2 Topic 3 — Energy Flow

Rate of Photosynthesis

Q4 Lucy investigated the **volume of oxygen** produced by pondweed at **different intensities of light**. Her results are shown in the table below.

Relative light intensity	1	2	3	4	5
Volume of oxygen produced in 10 minutes (ml)	12	25	13	48	61

a) What did Lucy measure by recording the volume of oxygen produced?

....

b) Plot a graph of her results.

c) i) One of Lucy's results is anomalous. Circle this point on the graph.

ii) Suggest an error Lucy might have made when she collected this result.

....

....

....

d) Describe the relationship shown on the graph between light intensity and photosynthesis rate.

....

....

e) Would you expect this relationship to continue if Lucy continued to increase the light intensity? Explain your answer.

....

....

Q5 Farmer Fred doesn't put his cows out during the winter because the grass is **not growing**.

a) Give **two** differences between summer and winter conditions that affect the rate of photosynthesis.

1. ....

2. ....

b) How are the rate of photosynthesis and the growth rate of the grass related?

....

....

B2 Topic 3 — Energy Flow

The Carbon Cycle

Q1 Complete the diagram below as instructed to show a **part** of the **carbon cycle**.

CO₂ in the air

plant   animal

a) Add an arrow or arrows labelled **P** to represent **photosynthesis**.

b) Add an arrow or arrows labelled **R** to represent **respiration**.

c) Add an arrow or arrows labelled **F** to represent **feeding**.

Q2 Answer the following questions to show how the **stages** in the **carbon cycle** are ordered.

a) Number the sentences below to show how carbon moves between the air and living things.

.... Animals eat the plants' carbon compounds.

....1....... Carbon dioxide in the air.

.... Plants and animals die.

.... Plants take in carbon dioxide for photosynthesis and make carbon compounds.

b) Add a point 5 to complete the cycle and show how carbon in dead organisms is returned to the air.

Point 5: ....

Q3 Answer the following questions about the **carbon cycle**.

a) What is the most common form of carbon found in the atmosphere?

....

b) What products do plants convert this carbon into?

....

c) How is the carbon in plants passed on through the food chain?

....

d) Give three things that can happen to dead plants and animals.

1. ....

2. ....

3. ....

B2 Topic 3 — Energy Flow

The Carbon Cycle

Q4 The diagram below shows one version of the **carbon cycle**.

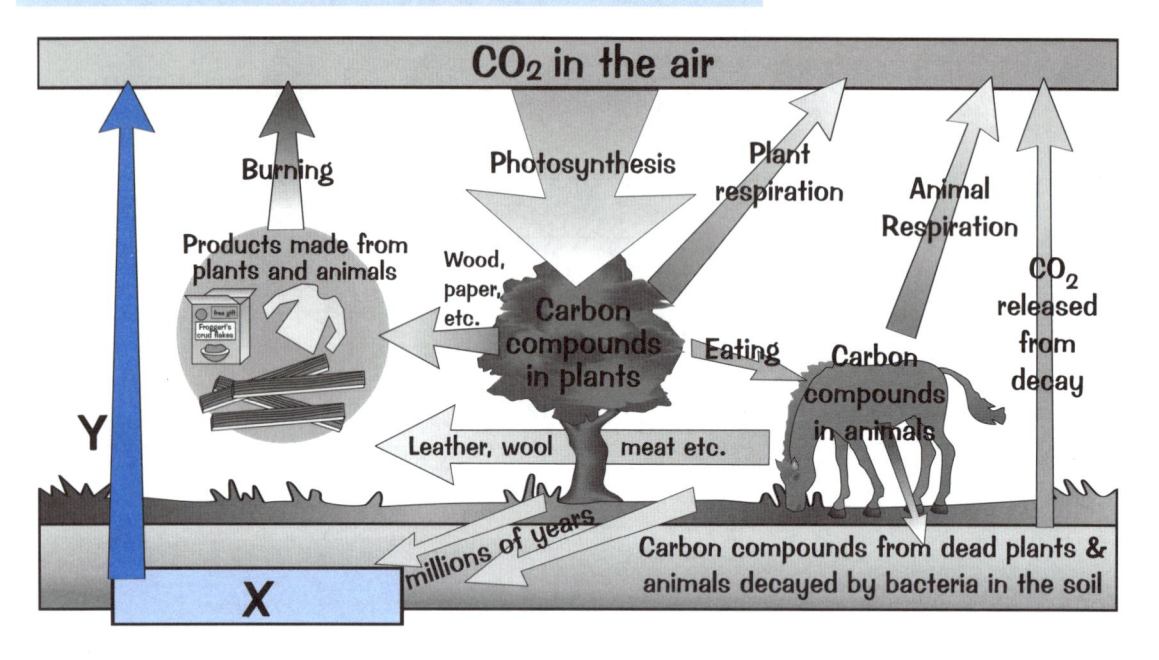

a) Name substance **X** shown on the diagram above. ....

b) Explain why substance **X** contains carbon.

....

....

c) Name the process labelled **Y** on the diagram above. ....

Q5 Nutrients are constantly **recycled**.

a) Name **three** elements (other than carbon) that are recycled in the environment.

....

b) Explain why **microorganisms** are important in recycling nutrients.

Don't just describe what the microorganisms do — explain why it's important.

....

....

....

Top Tip: Lots of substances are **recycled**, not just carbon. They enter organisms when they feed (or photosynthesise) and leave when they die, breathe or poo. That's the great circle of life for you.

B2 Topic 3 — Energy Flow

Minerals and Plants

Q1 A diagram of a **specialised plant cell** is shown on the right.

a) Name the type of cell shown. ....

b) What is the main function of this type of cell?

....

c) Why does this type of cell have the particular shape shown in the diagram?

....

d) What do plants use phosphates for?

....

e) Explain why minerals are **not** absorbed from the soil by the process of diffusion.

....

....

f) Explain how these specialised cells absorb minerals from the soil.
Use the words **active transport**, **concentration**, **respiration** and **energy** in your answer.

....

....

Q2 Rivers and lakes can be **polluted** by **fertilisers** that come from nearby farmland. This often results in the death of many fish.

a) Why are fertilisers essential to modern farming?

....

b) How does the fertiliser get into the rivers and lakes?

....

c) How does pollution by fertilisers cause fish to die?

....

....

d) What is the name given to this type of pollution by fertilisers? ....

e) What can farmers do to avoid causing this type of pollution?

....

....

B2 Topic 3 — Energy Flow

The Nitrogen Cycle

Q1 Circle the correct word to complete each statement below.

a) Nitrogen is need to make protein / carbohydrate / fat.

b) The percentage of nitrogen in the air is 94% / 21% / 78%.

c) Nitrogen is a reactive gas / an unreactive gas / a reactive liquid.

Q2 Match up each type of organism below with the correct way that it obtains nitrogen.

Plants	By breaking down dead organisms and animal waste
Animals	From nitrates in the soil
Bacteria	By eating other organisms

Q3 The nitrogen cycle is dependent on a number of different types of microorganism. Explain the role of each of the following types of bacteria in the nitrogen cycle.

Type of bacteria   **Role in the nitrogen cycle**

a) Decomposers ....

b) Nitrifying bacteria ....

c) Denitrifying bacteria ....

d) Nitrogen-fixing bacteria ....

Q4 Below is a diagram of the nitrogen cycle. Explain what is shown by the arrows labelled:

a) X ....

b) Y ....

c) Z ....

Q5 A farmer was told that if he planted legume plants his soil would be more fertile. Explain how the legume plants would increase the fertility of the soil.

....

....

B2 Topic 3 — Energy Flow

Life on Mars

Q1 From the list below, underline any factors that need to be **balanced** in a **biosphere**.

The amount of carbon dioxide produced and used.   The numbers of plants and animals.

Photosynthesis and respiration.   The amount of oxygen produced and used.   Fuel use and fuel production.

Q2 In the table, tick the columns to show in general which **organisms** carry out these **processes**.

Process	Animals	Plants	Microorganisms
Make food			
Produce oxygen			
Produce carbon dioxide			
Use oxygen			
Use carbon dioxide			

Q3 Read the passage below about an experiment in an **artificial biosphere** in Arizona, Biosphere 2, and then answer the questions which follow.

> For two years, biosphere 2 was sealed and monitored so that scientists could see if a safe equilibrium could be established within it. There was a problem with falling oxygen levels, and eventually the scientists had to pump in pure oxygen to keep the biosphere going. The scientists thought that the oxygen had been used up by microorganisms which had been put into the soil to encourage plant growth. However, the carbon dioxide levels would then have increased, but they had not. It was eventually found that concrete in the base of the facility had been absorbing CO_2, and this had reduced plant growth and caused a fall in oxygen levels.

a) What process in the microorganisms would have used up oxygen?

....

b) Why did the scientists expect an increase in CO_2 levels if the microorganisms were responsible?

....

c) How would introducing microorganisms 'encourage plant growth'?

....

....

d) Explain how the absorption of CO_2 by the concrete could have led to a fall in oxygen levels.

....

....

B2 Topic 3 — Energy Flow

Life on Mars

Q4 Look at the data showing details of the **atmosphere** and **temperature** range on **Earth** and **Mars**.

Planet	% oxygen in atmosphere	% CO_2 in atmosphere	Temperature range (°C)	Average temp. (°C)
Earth	21	0.04	-89.2 – +56.7	+15
Mars	0.13	95.32	-140 – +20	-63

a) From this data, give two factors that would make it hard for organisms from Earth to live on Mars.

....

....

b) One way that humans may be able to survive on Mars would be if they set up an artificial biosphere there. This has already been tried on Earth in **Biosphere 2** in Arizona.

  i) Do you think Biosphere 2 was useful for scientists planning a possible settlement on Mars? Give reasons for your answer.

  ....

  ....

  ii) Explain why it could be difficult to set up a similar biosphere on Mars.

  ....

  ....

Q5 Jane set up an experiment to see what effect **plants** and **animals** had on their **environment**. She used aquatic plants and snails, and bicarbonate indicator.

Bicarbonate indicator is red. If carbon dioxide is added, it goes **yellow**. If carbon dioxide is removed, it goes **purple**. Jane set up her experiment as shown in the diagram.

a) Give the colour you would expect the indicator to be after 24 hours in each tube.

A ....   B ....

C ....   D ....

b) Why did Jane include tube D in her experiment?

....

c) State **two** things that Jane should do in order to make this a fair test.

....

....

B2 Topic 3 — Energy Flow

There's Too Many People

Q1 The size of the Earth's **population** has an impact on our **environment**. The graph to the right shows how the world's human population has changed over the last 1000 years.

a) What was the approximate human population in 1800?

....

b) Tick the boxes to show whether a larger human population will increase or decrease the following things:

	Increase	Decrease
i) amount of raw materials available	☐	☐
ii) amount of waste	☐	☐
iii) amount of energy used	☐	☐
iv) amount of land available	☐	☐

Q2 Standards of living are **improving** in nearly all countries of the world. Explain how this is causing **environmental problems**.

....
....
....

Q3 The Earth receives energy from the **Sun**. It radiates much of this energy back out to space.

a) Explain the role of the greenhouse gases in keeping the Earth warm.

....
....
....

b) What would happen if there were no greenhouse gases?

....

c) In recent years the amount of greenhouse gases in the atmosphere has increased. Explain how this is thought to be leading to global warming.

....
....

B2 Topic 3 — Energy Flow

There's Too Many People

Q4 **Deforestation** increases the amount of **carbon dioxide** released into the atmosphere and decreases the amount removed.

a) Give two reasons why humans cut forests down.

....

....

b) Give two reasons why deforestation increases the concentration of atmospheric carbon dioxide.

....

....

c) Give one reason why deforestation reduces the amount of CO_2 removed from the atmosphere.

....

d) Give two other examples of human activities that release carbon dioxide into the atmosphere.

....

Q5 Global **waste production** has increased as population sizes and living standards have risen. To avoid **polluting** our environment, we need to **recycle** as much of this waste as possible.

The graph shows how the percentage of waste **recycled** in England grew between 1997 and 2004. A line has been drawn on the graph to show the trend in the data.

a) What percentage of waste was recycled in 2000? ....

b) If this trend continued, approximately what percentage of waste would be recycled in 2005?

....

c) State **two** ways that recycling waste helps to conserve the world's energy supplies.

....

....

B2 Topic 3 — Energy Flow

Climate Change and Food Distribution

Q1 Global warming may cause the seas to warm and **expand**, putting low lying areas at increased risk from **flooding**. This isn't the only possible consequence though — fill in the flow chart to show how temperatures might **decrease**.

Higher temperatures make ice melt.
Ocean currents are disrupted.

Some areas (maybe the UK) get colder.
Cold fresh water enters the ocean.

Q2 One UK newspaper said that **global warming** will be good for the UK because people will be able to have more **barbecues**. Do you think the newspaper is right? Explain your answer.

....

....

Q3 Many countries in the EU have **food surpluses**.

a) How have these food surpluses come about?

....

b) Suggest two problems that might occur if these surpluses were given to countries where there's a food shortage.

....

....

Q4 Southern Sudan, in north Africa, has one of the most severe **food shortages** on Earth. Reasons that have been given for this include the following:

There has been war and conflict for half a century.
Rainfall is low.
Agriculture is very basic.
It's one of the world's poorest countries.

a) How could wars have caused food shortages?

....

b) Suggest what could be done to help with the food shortage in the long term.

....

B2 Topic 3 — Energy Flow

Food Production

Q1 Three different **food chains** are shown here.

Grass → Cow → Human

Pondweed → Small fish → Salmon → Human

Wheat → Human

a) Circle the food chain that shows the most efficient production of food for humans.

b) Explain your choice.

....

Q2 Emma compared two ecosystems shown in the table. **Ecosystem A** was carefully controlled — the fish were kept in large cages and fed a special diet. Pesticides were used to kill unwanted pests. **Ecosystem B** was kept as natural as possible, with no cages, special diet or pest control.

Time in mths	Number of fish A	Number of fish B	Average size of fish (mm) A	Average size of fish (mm) B	Comments A	Comments B
0	200	200	362	348	200 fish introduced.	200 fish introduced.
2	189	191	368	392	A few initial losses due to change in habitat.	A few initial losses due to change in habitat. Initial growth rate seems fast.
4	188	152	374	423	Numbers stabilised. Water quality good.	High numbers of fish lice. Adults still growing well.
6	277	136	436	426	Breeding looks successful. Fish growth increasing.	Fish lice levels still high. Breeding has started. Growth rate decreasing.
8	349	172	359	372	End of breeding season. Adult fish growing well.	Breeding season. Fish numbers stabilising. Water pH 8.
10	338	184	401	382	Very few new fish have been lost.	Breeding season now over. Growth has slowed.
12	336	179	443	393	Population stable. Large, healthy fish.	Population stabilising. Water pH improved at 7.5.

a) Suggest why the average size of the fish drops so much in both ecosystems at 8 months.

....

b) What factors may have affected the growth rate and number of fish in Ecosystem B?

....

c) What conclusions could Emma draw from her investigation?

....

....

Q3 Jim wants to boost the growth of his vegetables, so he builds a **greenhouse**.

a) What is the main reason for the increase in plant growth inside a greenhouse?

....

b) Give two other conditions that can be altered artificially in a greenhouse to increase growth.

1. ....

2. ....

B2 Topic 3 — Energy Flow

B2 Topic 4 — Interdependence

Population Sizes

Q1 Draw lines below to link the **biological terms** on the left with any **examples** on the right.

- Adaptation
- Competition
- Predation

A lion eats an antelope.

Plants of different species in a meadow all need light.

Grasses that grow in dry areas have longer roots.

A bear eats a fish.

Animals in a rock pool all get their oxygen from the water.

Q2 Look at the diagram of a **food web** and answer the questions that follow.

a) Which organism is the whole food web dependent on? Explain your answer.

....

....

....

b) Name two organisms which you would expect to be competing with each other. Explain your answer.

....

....

....

....

c) Suggest what might happen to the population of the spiders if pesticides killed off most of the greenfly. Give a reason for your answer.

....

....

Q3 **Hawks** are large **predators** found at the tops of their food webs. A hawk is shown in the diagram.

Give three ways that a hawk is adapted to being a carnivore.

Eyes at front of head allow good judgment of distance
Sharp beak with hooked end
Large, strong wings
Sharp claws
Thick layers of feathers provide insulation

....

....

....

....

Population Sizes

Q4 It is common for the males of many species to set up **territories** (areas where they are the only male). They will fight off any other males that try to enter their territory.

Suggest why having a territory is a useful adaptation.

....

....

Q5 **Herring** and **cod** are fish that are caught for food in the North Sea. The graph shows the size of the fish populations (measured in biomass) over the last thirty years. Herring fishing in the North Sea was **banned** between 1978 and 1982.

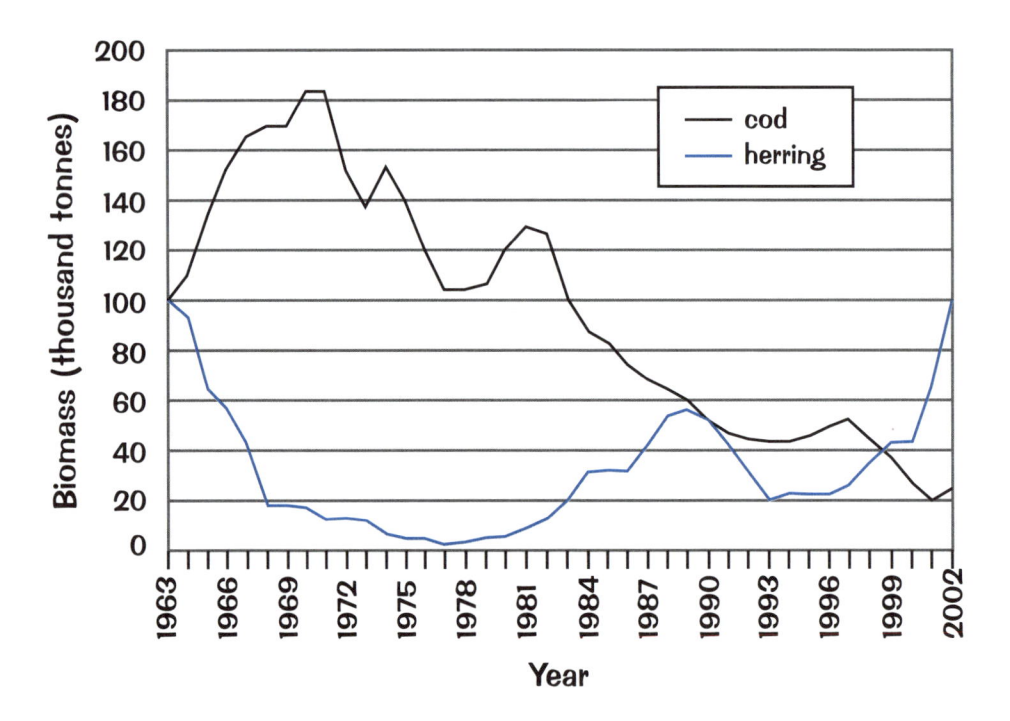

a) Between what years was the **cod** population at its highest level? ....

b) Describe the changes seen in the number of **herring** in the North Sea between 1963 and 1989.

....

....

c) Suggest an explanation for the changes you described above.

....

....

d) Use this data to suggest **one** thing that could be done to help the cod population survive.

....

B2 Topic 4 — Interdependence

Extreme Environments

Q1 The picture below shows an **angler fish**. Angler fish live in very **deep seas**, where sunlight cannot penetrate.

- Luminous organ that glows in the dark
- Huge mouth with sharp teeth

a) What conditions make the deep sea a hostile environment?

....

....

b) Suggest how the following features help the angler fish to stay alive in its environment:

i) The luminous organ on its head.

....

ii) Its huge mouth.

....

Q2 There is usually a much higher density of life found on the seabed around **hot vents**.

a) Give two things that are provided by the hot vents that make it easier for life to exist around them.

....

b) The food webs around hot vents are not based on photosynthesis, unlike most others on Earth.

i) Name the process that hot vent food webs rely on.

....

ii) Briefly explain how this process works.

....

....

c) Name the type of organism found at the bottom of hot vent food webs.

....

B2 Topic 4 — Interdependence

Extreme Environments

Q3 List three difficulties that organisms living at **high altitude** face.

1. ....
2. ....
3. ....

Q4 When a major **sports event** is held in a country that is at a **high altitude**, the participants usually go out to the country some time before the event in order to '**acclimatise**' to the lower levels of **oxygen**. The graph below shows how their **fitness** changes after arrival at high altitude.

a) Describe the change in fitness shown by the graph.

....
....

b) Suggest how a lack of oxygen might lead to a drop in performance at a sports event.

....
....

c) Athletes that have acclimatised have more red blood cells. How will this help them to perform?

....

Q5 Penguins living in the **Antarctic** have to survive very low temperatures. They have feathers, which trap air to form an **insulating layer**, and a thick layer of **fat** under their skin. The only places on their bodies that do not have a thick insulating layer are the feet and the flippers.

a) The muscles that operate a penguin's feet and flippers are not actually in these parts of its body, but in the main part of the body. Explain why this is important.

....
....

b) The penguin needs these muscles to propel it through the water. Suggest why many of the animals found in the Antarctic are adapted for swimming.

....
....

Top Tip: **Extreme environments** are places with conditions that few species can cope with. For those that can, life's no picnic but on the plus side there's **very little competition** from other species.

B2 Topic 4 — Interdependence

Air Pollution — CO_2 and CO

Q1 **Exhaust fumes** from cars and lorries often contain **carbon monoxide**.

a) Why is this more likely to be formed in engines than if the fuel was burnt in the open air?

....

....

b) Why is carbon monoxide so dangerous?

....

Q2 Look at the graph and then answer the questions below.

a) Describe the **trend** shown by the graph.

....

....

....

....

b) What is the main cause of this trend?

....

c) What effect do many scientists believe the trend shown in the graph is having on the Earth's average temperature?

....

Q3 The maps show the results of a study into **carbon monoxide pollution** in an area of England.

Pollution by carbon monoxide: dark blue = high, pale blue = medium, white = low.

Towns and villages in study area (in dark grey) with road connections.

a) Describe and explain the pattern of pollution shown on the maps.

....

....

b) What evidence is there that motor vehicles are a major source of carbon monoxide pollution?

....

B2 Topic 4 — Interdependence

Interpreting Data: Climate Change

Q1 Two university students carried out **observations**. Student A noticed that a glacier was melting. Student B noticed that daffodils flowered earlier in 2006 than in 2005. Both students concluded that this was due to **global warming**. Are they right? Explain your answer.

....

....

Q2 Scientists are collecting **evidence** to try to support or disprove the **theory** of global warming.

Give examples of the sort of data that scientists are collecting about climate change.

....

....

Q3 Many scientists think that the Earth is **warming up**. The graph shows the mean temperature between **1961** and **1990**, and how the temperature has differed from it over the last **300 years**.

a) Does this graph support the theory that the Earth is getting warmer? Explain your answer.

....

....

b) What do some scientists think is responsible for this increase in temperature?

....

....

In order to study possible global warming, scientists have looked at the Earth's temperature over a very long period. The graph on the left shows the temperature variations over the last 2000 years (older temperatures are worked out by studying the effects they had on bodies of water, glaciers and living things).

c) Some scientists believe that the current temperature rise is the result of normal long-term temperature variation. Look at the graph and explain whether or not it supports this idea.

....

....

B2 Topic 4 — Interdependence

Air Pollution — Acid Rain

Q1   Draw lines to match each sentence with the best ending.

The main cause of acid rain is   acid rain.

Acid rain kills trees and   sulphuric acid.

Limestone buildings and statues are affected by   acidifies lakes.

In clouds sulphur dioxide reacts with water to make   sulphur dioxide.

Q2   Use the words and phrases below to complete the paragraph.

nitric   sulphur dioxide   carbon dioxide   sulphuric   nitrogen oxides   acid rain
When fossil fuels are burned, ... is produced. This causes the greenhouse effect. The gas .... is also produced. This comes from sulphur impurities in the fuel. When it combines with moisture in the air .... acid is produced and falls as acid rain. In the high temperature inside a car engine, nitrogen and oxygen from the air react together to produce .... These react with moisture to produce .... acid, which is another cause of acid rain.

Q3   Ben was investigating the effect of **acid rain** on the **germination** of cress seeds. He set up six sets of apparatus (as shown in the diagram), five with a different **strength of acid** in the container and one with water only. He left them for three days and then calculated the percentage of seeds that had germinated. His results are shown on the graph.

   a)   Estimate the percentage germination
          if Ben had used 0.4 M acid. ....

   b)   What conclusions could Ben draw from his experiment?

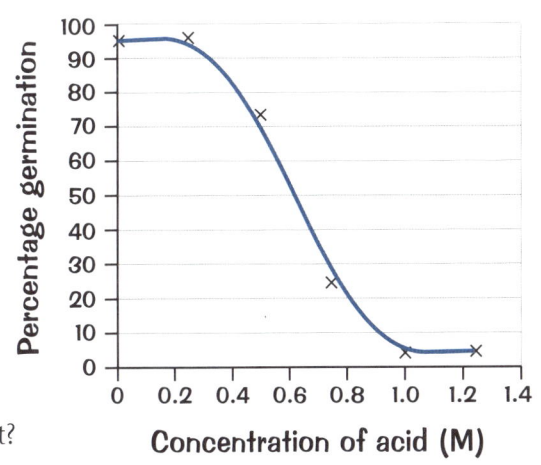

   ....

   ....

   ....

   c)   Why did Ben set up an experiment with just water and no acid?

   ....

B2 Topic 4 — Interdependence

Water Pollution

Q1 Suggest one way that each of the following **pollutants** can get into rivers and streams.

a) Pesticides.
....

b) Oil.
....

c) Metals.
....

Q2 This is a **food chain** based around a stream.

Algae → Water louse → Dragonfly nymph → Water shrew → Kestrel

a) If the stream is polluted by a pesticide such as DDT, which of the organisms in the food chain is most likely to suffer?
....

b) Explain your answer to part **a)**.
....
....

Q3 Scientists tested the water in a river before and after it passed a farm. The farm was suspected of polluting the river with **sewage**. Direct measurements of the levels of **nitrogen**, **phosphorus** and **oxygen** were taken. Complete the table below by ticking the appropriate boxes to show how you would expect the water to be different after passing the farm if it was polluting the river.

Chemical	Level rises	Level stays the same	Level falls
Nitrogen			
Phosphorus			
Oxygen			

B2 Topic 4 — Interdependence

Water Pollution

Q4 Environment officers monitored two **polluted rivers**. One had been polluted with **fertiliser**, the other with a **heavy metal poison**. Numbers of two insect species were counted in the rivers — **rat-tailed maggots**, which survive well in oxygen-depleted water, and **stonefly larvae**, which need a high level of oxygen.

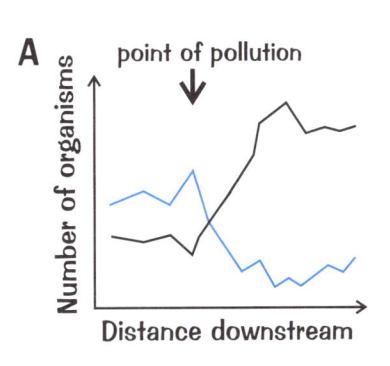

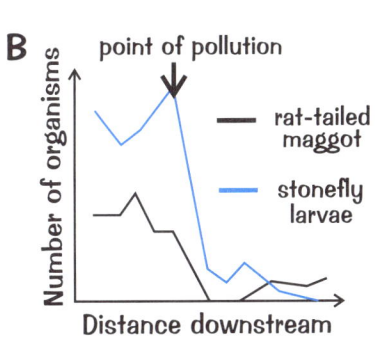

A — point of pollution — Number of organisms vs Distance downstream

B — point of pollution — Number of organisms vs Distance downstream — rat-tailed maggot, stonefly larvae

a) Complete the following: The river polluted with **fertiliser** is shown on graph ....

The river polluted with a **heavy metal** is shown on graph ....

b) Explain the differences seen in the graphs for the two rivers.

....

....

....

Q5 The graph shows the numbers of serious incidents of **water pollution** in different areas of a European country between 2002-2005.

a) Which area had the least pollution incidents

i) in 2002? ....

ii) in 2003? ....

b) Does the graph give evidence for a fall in water pollution between 2004 and 2005? Explain your answer.

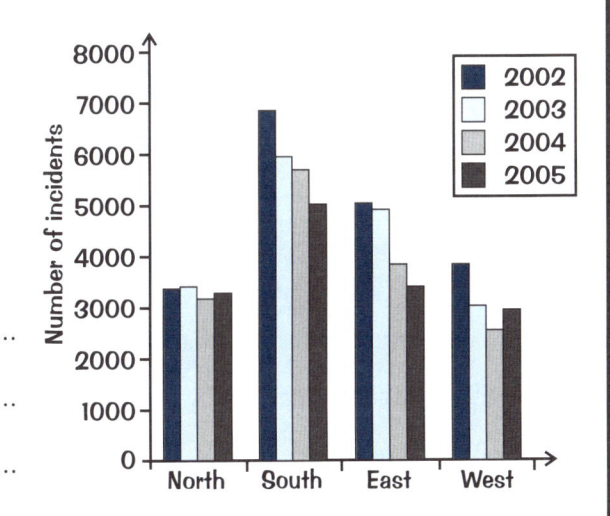

....

....

....

c) Suggest a reason why there are many more pollution incidents in the South of this country than in the West.

....

....

Top Tip: A **direct measurement** of water pollution is made by testing a sample to check the levels of different chemicals. An **indirect measurement** is made by looking at what's living in the water.

B2 Topic 4 — Interdependence

Living Indicators

Q1 Mayfly larvae and sludge worms are often studied to see how much sewage is in water.

a) What is the name for an organism used in this way?

....

Juanita recorded the number of each species in water samples taken at three different distances downstream from a sewage outlet. Her results are shown below.

Distance (m)	No. of mayfly larvae	No. of sludge worms
20	3	20
40	11	14
60	23	7

b) State **one** thing that she would have to do to make this experiment a fair test.

....

c) What can you conclude about the two organisms from these results?

....

....

....

Q2 Tick the right boxes to say whether the sentences below are **true** or **false**.   True   False

a) All pollution comes from factories and power stations.

b) Lichens can be used as indicator species for air pollution.

c) Lichens prefer areas of low air quality.

d) The number of cases of skin cancer is also an indicator of pollution.

e) Skin cancer is caused by high levels of sulphur dioxide in the atmosphere.

f) Damage to the ozone layer means it absorbs more radiation from the Sun.

Q3 Underline any substance known to damage the **ozone layer**.

Methane   Carbon dioxide

  CFCs   Sulphur dioxide

B2 Topic 4 — Interdependence

Living Indicators

Q4 Use the words in the box to complete the following passage about the thinning **ozone layer**.

| infra-red | aerosols | oxygen | CFCs | cars | ozone |
| ultraviolet | skin cancer | nitrous oxides | lung cancer |

The Earth's atmosphere has a layer of .... in it. This layer protects the planet from .... radiation. Over the last thirty years there has been a thinning of the layer due to air pollution by ...., which are gases used in ...., air conditioning and refrigerator coolants. The thinning of this layer is a concern because the radiation that gets through can cause ....

Q5 The number of species of **lichen** living in an area can be used as an **indicator** of how **clean** the air is there. Scientists did a survey of the number of lichens found on gravestones at different distances from a city centre. The results are shown below:

Distance from city centre (km)	No. of species found on ten gravestones
0	12
2	13
6	22
16	29
20	15
24	35

No. of species of lichen

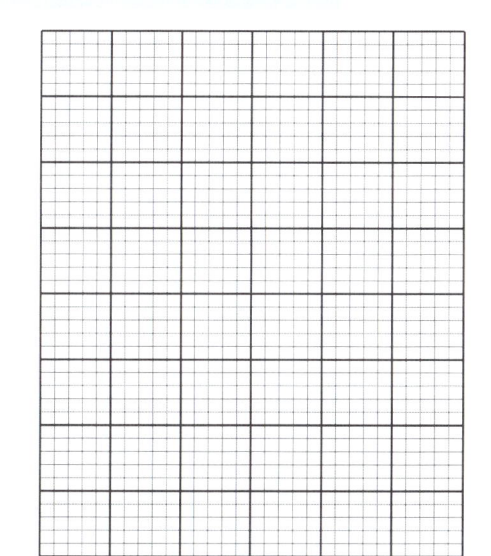

Distance from city centre (km)

a) Draw a graph of this data on the grid provided.

b) State two precautions that the scientists would have needed to take when doing the experiment in order to ensure that the test was fair.

....

....

c) What **general trend** is shown by the data?

....

....

d) The result at 20 km is **anomalous** — it doesn't fit the general trend. Suggest a possible reason for this.

....

B2 Topic 4 — Interdependence

Conservation

Q1 One of the aims of **conservation** is to maintain the **biodiversity** in a habitat.

Explain what is meant by **biodiversity**, and why is it important to preserve biodiversity in a habitat.

....

....

Q2 The stocks of **cod** in the waters around Britain have greatly decreased. Most of the fish caught are about two years old. Cod mature and start to **reproduce** at about 4–5 years old. It has been suggested that using nets with a **larger mesh size** might help to conserve the stocks.

a) Why would it be better if fish were caught **after** they had reached their reproductive age?

....

b) Why might increasing the **mesh size** of fishing nets help to conserve stocks?

....

c) Give one reason why it is important to preserve the stocks of cod in the waters around Britain.

....

Q3 Suggest **three** methods that can be used to conserve **woodland**.

....

....

Q4 The **elephant population** in an African national park (a conservation area) is growing rapidly. Large numbers of elephants **damage** their habitat, trampling plants that other animals need for food. During the last century, the elephants were 'culled' for a time (the 'extra' elephants were shot). The growth of the elephant population is shown in the graph.

a) From the graph, suggest when the 'cull' started and ended.

....

b) The national park was set up in 1905.
Suggest why the elephant population was so low at the time.

....

c) Suggest **one** alternative way of reducing the elephant population without 'culling'.

....

B2 Topic 4 — Interdependence

Recycling

Q1 Tick the boxes to show which of the following are good reasons for **recycling metals**.

☐ The recycling process gives many metals useful new properties.
☐ It uses less energy and therefore less fossil fuel.
☐ The metal produced is purer and so of a higher quality.
☐ Less carbon dioxide is produced as a result.

Q2 Most plastics are **not** biodegradable.

Biodegradable means that something can rot.

a) What problems does this cause for the environment?

....
....

b) How can you minimise this environmental problem when using objects made from plastics?

....

c) Things are often made from plastics because they are cheap. Why might this change in the future?

....
....

Q3 There are important **benefits** of recycling, but it is still **not** a perfect solution.

a) Explain how recycling materials helps to conserve the world's energy resources.

....
....

b) State three ways in which the recycling process uses energy.

1. ....
2. ....
3. ....

B2 Topic 4 — Interdependence

Recycling

Q4 The diagram shows the changes in the amounts of different materials **recycled** through **kerbside collection schemes** from 2002–2004.

a) Estimate the increase in total tonnes of materials collected.

....

b) The graph shows an increase in the collection of 'comingled materials'. This is waste containing a mixture of different recyclable materials. Suggest one **disadvantage** of collecting such waste.

....

c) Explain why this data **can't** be used as evidence that more material in total was recycled in the UK from 2003–2004 than from 2002–2003.

....

....

d) Suggest one advantage of kerbside collection schemes over recycling banks (central sites where people bring their rubbish to be recycled).

....

Q5 Explain each of the following statements about **recycling**.

a) Recycling **glass** can help to conserve fossil fuels.

....

....

....

b) Recycling **paper** can help to reduce global warming.

Think about the carbon cycle.

....

....

....

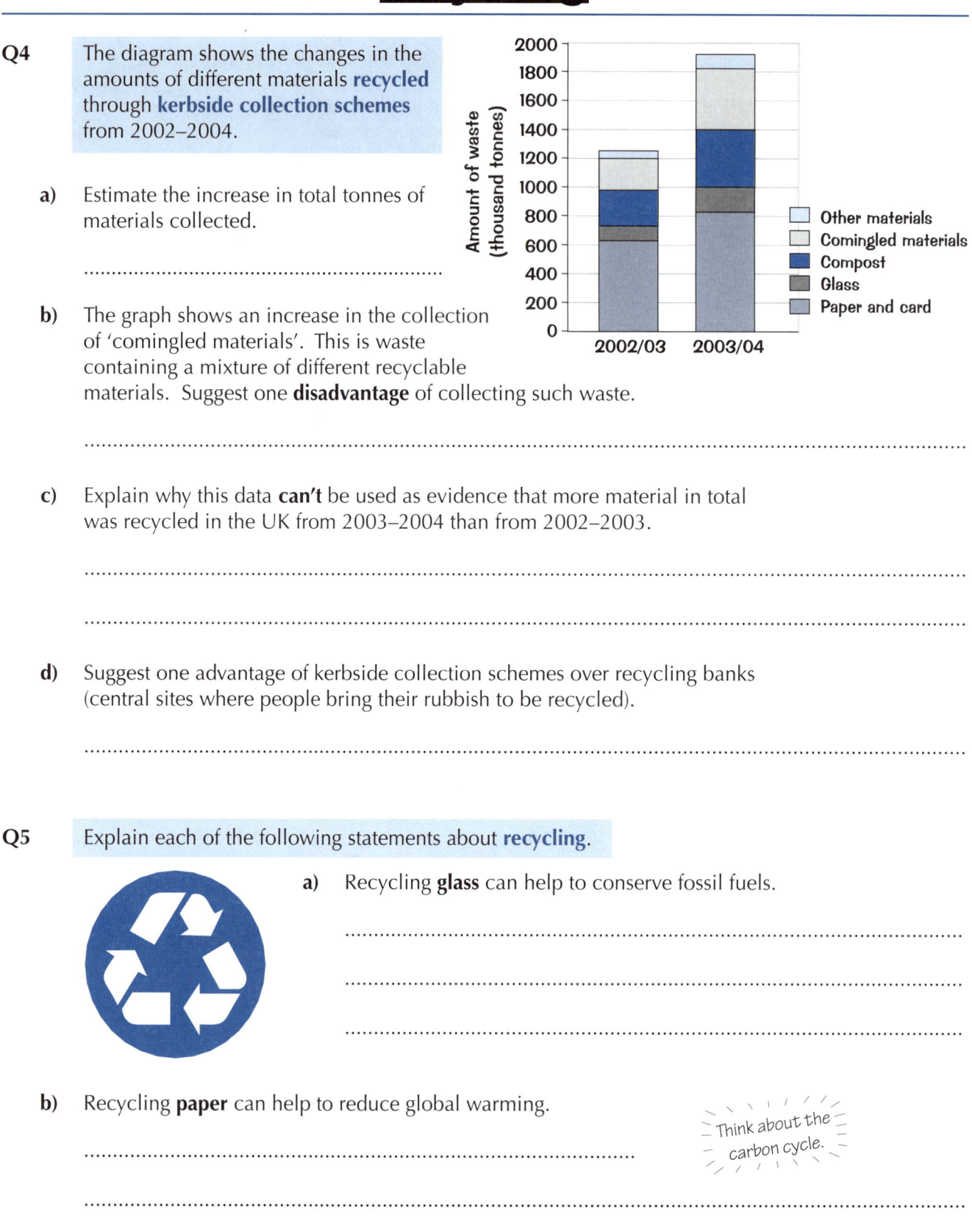

Top Tip: The UK isn't too great at recycling — we're getting better, but still languishing far behind other European countries. Collection schemes are making things easier, so no more excuses.

B2 Topic 4 — Interdependence

Mixed Questions — B2 Topics 3 & 4

Q1 The diagram shows a **plant**, A, growing in a **tropical rainforest**.

a) Which factor is most likely to limit the rate of photosynthesis in plant A? Explain your answer.

....

....

b) Give two other factors that often limit the rate of photosynthesis in plants.

....

c) Name one mineral that plants need in order to photosynthesise. ....

d) Plants use a process called active transport to take minerals into their roots. Explain what this is.

....

....

Q2 **Carbon** is continually being **recycled** from one form to another. The **carbon cycle** shown below is incomplete.

Name the processes A, B, C, D, E and F.

A ....

B ....

C ....

D ....

E ....

F ....

Q3 **Legumes** are plants that have nodules on their roots containing **nitrogen-fixing bacteria**.

a) Plants absorb nitrogen compounds from the soil. What is the name of these nitrogen compounds?

....

b) Explain why plants can't get their nitrogen directly from the air.

....

c) The legumes and the nitrogen-fixing bacteria have a mutualistic relationship. Explain fully what this means.

....

....

B2 Topic 4 — Interdependence

Mixed Questions — B2 Topics 3 & 4

Q4 The Earth's **human population** has been **increasing** more and more rapidly for many years.

a) Explain how the growing population is thought to be altering the Earth's **climate**.

....

....

....

....

b) It has been suggested that if the Earth's population increases to a completely unsustainable level, it might be possible to colonise Mars.

  i) Explain why the natural environment on Mars could not support life.

  ....

  ii) How could life from Earth survive on Mars?

  ....

Q5 The graph shows how the **populations** of **snowy owls** and **lemmings** in a community vary over time.

Describe and explain the reasons for the population trends shown on the graph.

....

....

....

....

Q6 The picture shows an animal that is **adapted** to survive in an **extreme environment**. Its fur is white and it is a carnivore.

a) Suggest the type of habitat where you would expect to find this animal.

....

b) Give three features that the animal has evolved to cope in this climate and briefly explain how each feature helps the animal to survive.

....

....

....

Mixed Questions — B2 Topics 3 & 4

Q7 Human activity causes various types of **air pollution**. Four common air pollutants are:

CO_2 CO SO_2 NO_x

Each statement below refers to one or more of these pollutants. Indicate which one(s) in the space provided.

a) May be released when fossil fuels are burnt. ....

b) Amount in the atmosphere is increased by deforestation. ....

c) Linked with global warming and climate change. ....

d) A poisonous gas that prevents red blood cells carrying oxygen. ....

e) Cause acid rain when they mix with clouds. ....

f) Comes from impurities in fossil fuels. ....

Q8 **Water pollution** can be measured both **directly** and **indirectly**.

a) Explain what each of these methods involves.

....

....

b) A sample of water is taken from two different streams. The sample from stream A contains 19 organisms of two different species. The sample from stream B contain 36 organisms of eight different species. Which stream do you think is the more polluted? Explain your answer.

....

....

Q9 Woodland Industries is a company that produces **wood** for **manufacturing paper**. They have introduced several measures to ensure that the woodland habitats used are **conserved**.

a) Explain what each of the following measures involves:

i) Reforestation ....

ii) Coppicing ....

iii) Replacement planting ....

b) These measures allow Woodland Industries to produce a constant supply of paper without losing the woodland habitat. Explain why it would still be worthwhile to recycle the paper they make.

....

....

c) One of the English woods owned by Woodland Industries contains several old oak trees. The company has agreed with the local council not to fell the trees because they are part of England's 'cultural heritage'. Explain what this means.

....

B2 Topic 4 — Interdependence

B3 Topic 1 — Biotechnology

Microorganisms and Food

Q1 **Biotechnology** has been used for many years in the **food industry**.

a) Name **two** types of microorganisms that are widely used in the production of food.

1. .... 2. ....

b) **Fermentation** by microorganisms is an important process in the food industry

i) Explain what is meant by **fermentation**

....

ii) What is a **fermenter**?

....

Q2 Complete the passage about **yoghurt making** by filling in the gaps using the words below.

cooled   ferment   flavours   clot   pasteurised   lactic acid   bacteria   incubated

To make yoghurt, milk is .... to kill off any unwanted microorganisms, then .... Next, a starter culture of .... is added and the mixture is .... The bacteria .... the lactose sugar into .... This causes the milk to .... and form yoghurt. .... such as fruit are then sometimes added.

Q3 Number these steps in the manufacture of **soy sauce** to give the correct order.

.... fermentation by *Aspergillus*   .... pasteurisation
.... filtering   .... fermentation by yeast
.... soya beans and roasted wheat are mixed .... fermentation by *Lactobacillus*

Q4 Some people take **prebiotics** to promote the growth of **'good' bacteria** in the gut.

a) What are prebiotics?

....

b) Why are humans and 'bad' bacteria unable to digest prebiotics?

....

c) Give two natural sources of prebiotics.

1. .... 2. ....

Microorganisms and Food

Q5 **Microorganisms** are used in the manufacture of various **additives** and **supplements**.
Draw lines to match each of the microorganisms below with the substance it is used to help make.

a) *Acetobacter*   monosodium glutamate

b) *Aspergillus niger*   low-calorie sweetener

c) *Corynebacterium glutamicum*   vitamin C supplement

d) *Saccharomyces cerevisiae*   citric acid

Q6 Scientists did an experiment into the effectiveness of **stanol esters** in lowering people's **blood cholesterol**. They asked two groups of 100 people each to use a special spread instead of butter. Group A's spread was based on vegetable oil. Group B's spread was exactly the same, except that it contained large amounts of stanol esters. The cholesterol levels of each group were measured before the start of the experiment, and again after six months. The results are shown in the table.

	Group A / units	Group B / units
Mean blood cholesterol at start	6.3	6.4
Mean blood cholesterol after 6 mths	6.1	5.5

a) Explain the purpose of Group A.

....

b) Why did the scientists use 100 people in each group?

....

c) What precautions should the scientists have taken when choosing people for this experiment, to make sure that their results were valid?

....

d) Why is it necessary to measure the blood cholesterol before the experiment as well as at the end?

....

e) Explain why it is important that people with high blood cholesterol take steps to lower it.

....

f) Explain how bacteria are involved in making spreads such as that used by group B.

....

....

Top Tips: Remember some bacteria are 'bad' and can cause disease but there are also 'good' bacteria. Everyone has 'good' bacteria in their guts — they're really important for digestion.

B3 Topic 1 — Biotechnology

Microorganisms and Food

Q7 Different substances are added to foods for different reasons. Draw lines to match each of these **food additives** to its **function**.

a) Chymosin   sweetener

b) Fructose   flavouring

c) MSG   preservative

d) Vitamin C   clotting agent

Q8 The Complacent Cow Company makes **cheese** from cow's milk using an **enzyme** that comes from **genetically modified yeast**. They claim that they "make cheese without cruelty to animals".

a) Name the enzyme that the Complacent Cow Company uses. ....

b) Describe briefly how yeasts can be made to produce this enzyme.

....

c) Explain why the Complacent Cow Company's cheese might be popular with vegetarians, but cheese from other companies might not be.

....

....

Q9 A sweet manufacturer uses an enzyme produced by **yeast** to convert **sucrose** into **fructose**.

a) Name the enzyme involved in this process.

....

b) Explain the purpose of converting sucrose into fructose.

....

....

Q10 Consider the **commercial manufacture** of the **food products** listed in the box below.

| carrageenan | citric acid | fructose | soy sauce | stanols | yoghurt |

From this list, choose the product or products:

a) used as a preservative. ....

b) depending on fungi for production. ....

c) depending on bacteria for production. ....

d) not requiring microorganisms for production. ....

B3 Topic 1 — Biotechnology

Diet and Obesity

Q1 Complete the following sentences to show the **functions** in the body of different **nutrients**.

a) Protein is needed for .... and ....

b) Carbohydrates provide much of your ....

c) Fats are used to form cell .... and .... hormones.

Q2 **Kwashiorkor** is a condition caused by lack of **protein** in the diet.

Why is this condition most common in poorer developing countries?

....

Q3 **Vitamins** and **minerals** are two **essential nutrients** needed in the diet. Explain why each of the following examples are needed, and what the health consequences could be if they are lacking.

a) **Vitamin C** is needed for ....

A lack of vitamin C could lead to ....

b) **Iron** is needed for ....

A lack of iron could lead to ....

Q4 **Fifty** men and **fifty** women were asked whether they thought they were **obese**.
Each was then given a medical examination to **check** whether they were actually obese.

	Thought they were obese	Actually obese
No. of women	9	16
No. of men	5	11

a) What percentage of women in this survey were obese? ....

b) What are the most common **causes** of obesity in developed countries?

....

c) Is an obesity study based on data from **questionnaires** likely to be accurate? Explain your answer.

....

....

d) Underline any health problems in the list below that have been linked to obesity.

heart disease   hepatitis   influenza   cancers   scurvy   diabetes

---

Top Tips: Don't forget, **malnutrition** is when the diet you eat isn't balanced — which includes eating **too much**, as well as too little or not enough of certain things.

B3 Topic 1 — Biotechnology

Genetically Modifying Plants

Q1 Use the words provided to fill in the blanks in the passage below.

bacteria   herbicide   insecticide   plants   vector

Agrobacterium tumefaciens and *Bacillus thuringiensis* are both .... that can be used in biotechnology. *Agrobacterium tumefaciens* can be used as a .... to insert a gene for .... resistance into plants. *Bacillus thuringiensis* produces a natural .... and the gene for this can be cut out and inserted into ....

Q2 **Famine** and **malnutrition** have various causes, and **biotechnology** can help to find solutions for some of them. Look at the descriptions of **genetically modified plants** below, and in each case say which **cause of famine** or malnutrition it could provide a solution to.

e.g. Plants that can tolerate water loss. ....*drought*.........

a) Plants that can fix their own nitrogen. ....

b) Plants that contain extra vitamins. ....

c) Plants that produce their own insecticide. ....

Q3 These are some statements that different people made about **GM plants**. In each case, say whether they are making an argument **for** or **against** GM technology.

a) "Genes newly inserted into crop plants, for example for pest-resistance, may spread to nearby wild plants." — Gregory Greene, conservationist. ....

b) "**Some people could develop allergic reactions to foods that have been genetically modified.**" — Jermaine Eaton, nutritionist. ....

c) "We can produce rice plants containing toxins that are harmful to locusts but not to people." — Veronica Speedwell, biotechnology consultant. ....

d) "**By using herbicide-resistant crops on my land, I can kill all the weeds in my field with a single dose of all-purpose herbicide.**" — Ed Jones, farmer. ....

e) "Investing in improving traditional agricultural methods will improve yields more than investment in GM technology." — Abigail Singh, relief worker. ....

Q4 Some stages in the production of a **herbicide-resistant maize plant** are listed below. Put the stages in the correct order.

A The herbicide-resistance gene is inserted into *Agrobacterium tumefaciens*.

B Infected cells from maize are grown in a medium containing herbicide.

C The gene that makes a wild corn plant resistant to herbicide is identified.

D *Agrobacterium tumefaciens* is allowed to infect a maize plant.

E The herbicide-resistance gene is cut out from a wild corn plant.

Order: ....

B3 Topic 1 — Biotechnology

Genetically Modifying Plants

Q5 Unicourt Biotech, an American company, has developed a new **GM rice** that gives a **higher yield** than ordinary rice and which is also **resistant to diseases**.

Ruritasia is a poor island in South-East Asia. The rice would grow well there, but some of the local farmers **don't** want to use it.

a) Why might it be good for the people of Ruritasia if they used the GM rice?

....

....

b) The people of Ruritasia have several different objections to the use of GM rice. Explain each of the objections given below:

i) It's a danger to people's health.

....

ii) It's a danger to local habitats.

....

iii) It causes dependence on a foreign company.

....

....

c) If the climate in Ruritasia changed, resulting in lack of rain, what kind of GM crop could be used?

....

Q6 **Golden rice** was developed in order to increase the amount of **vitamin A** that could be obtained from a rice crop. It is estimated that a person would only have to eat **144 g** of golden rice per day in order to receive the recommended daily allowance of vitamin A, compared with **2.3 kg** of natural basmati rice.

a) Golden rice does not actually contain much more vitamin A than basmati rice. Explain how Golden rice increases the amount of vitamin A that a person receives.

....

....

b) It has been suggested that Golden rice would be very useful as a crop in developing countries. Explain why it might be particularly useful in such countries.

....

....

B3 Topic 1 — Biotechnology

Genetically Modifying Plants

Q7 A crop plant had been genetically modified to make it **resistant to herbicides**. Some people were **concerned** that, as a result, wild grasses growing nearby might also become resistant to herbicides. Scientists decided to check whether this had happened.

The scientists sprayed herbicide onto 100 plants in an area next to the GM crop, and onto 100 plants from a second area far away from the GM crop. The results are shown in the table.

Number of grass plants dying after spraying	
In area next to GM crop	In area far away from GM crop
83	85

a) Explain the reason for testing a group of plants that had not been growing near the GM crop.

....

b) How could the scientists have made the results of this experiment **more reliable**?

....

c) The scientists decided that there was no significant difference between the two groups of plants. Explain whether you agree or disagree with this conclusion.

....

....

d) If the scientists are right in their conclusion, does this prove that the concerns about genes for resistance spreading are unfounded? Explain your answer.

....

....

....

e) If wild grasses become resistant to herbicides, what **problems** might this cause?

....

....

f) Crop plants can be genetically modified so that they grow better under various conditions, or so that their nutritional value is improved. Suggest **two** other reasons why a crop might be modified.

....

....

Top Tips: If GM organisms **don't** cause any unexpected problems, then all's fine and dandy. But if it turns out that they **do**, it could be a problem, as they're **already** being used in some countries.

B3 Topic 1 — Biotechnology

New Treatments — Drugs

Q1 The table shows some different **drugs** that can be extracted from **plants** and their **uses**. Fill in the blanks to complete it.

DRUG	EXTRACTED FROM	USES
artemisinin	*Artemisia annua* plant	
salicin		painkiller
	Pacific yew tree	
quinine		anti-malarial

Q2 When companies produce a **new drug**, they are allowed to **patent** it. Then they can control the **price** at which they sell it. Some people think that this system is a good idea, but others don't.

For each of the quotes below, say whether you think the person is **for** or **against** the patent system.

a) "It costs millions of pounds to do the research needed to create a new drug." ....

b) "Drug companies are making money out of people's suffering." ....

c) "Less economically developed countries can't afford to buy essential new drugs." ....

d) "Companies need an incentive to invest in the development of new drugs." ....

e) "Companies that make copies of new drugs can provide them more cheaply." ....

Q3 The graph shows the amount of **money** spent on buying **drugs** by the health services of two countries with similar population sizes.

a) How has spending by country A changed between 1990 and 2006?

....

....

b) Give **two** possible reasons for this trend.

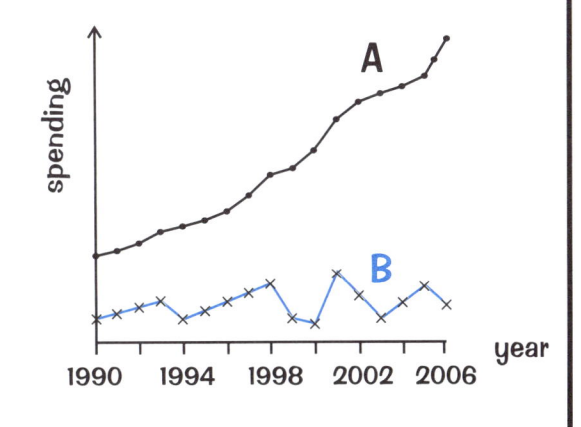

....

c) Suggest why the spending by country **B** does not show a similar trend.

....

d) Explain how abandoning the patent system for new drugs might help country B.

....

....

e) Explain why abandoning the patent system might **not** be a good idea for people in either country.

....

B3 Topic 1 — Biotechnology

New Treatments — Using Genetics

Q1 **Genetically modified bacteria** can be made to produce **human insulin**. There are several **advantages** of this over using insulin from animals. Explain each of the advantages given below.

a) Safety ....

b) Quantity ....

c) Economic advantages ....

d) Suitability for vegetarians and vegans ....

e) Quality ....

Q2 Use the words provided in the box to fill in the blanks in the passage below.

design   genome   genomics   medicine   predispose   prevent

The complete genetic make-up of an organism is its ....
The study of this is called ...., and it could be useful in
................................., to develop treatments. Some people have genes
which .... them to certain diseases. Identifying these
genes in a person may help to .... the diseases ever
developing. One day, it may also help doctors to ....
specific drugs which suit an individual patient's particular genetic make-up.

Q3 It is known that if a woman is carrying a certain **gene**, her chances of developing **breast cancer** before the age of 45 are **significantly higher** than the chances of a woman without this gene developing breast cancer before this age.

a) If a woman is a carrier of this gene:

i) suggest two advantages of her knowing that she has the gene.

....

....

ii) suggest one disadvantage of her knowing.

....

b) Explain how knowing more about this gene could help scientists improve the treatment available.

....

....

....

B3 Topic 1 — Biotechnology

Reproductive Technology

Q1 Read the paragraph below, and then answer the questions that follow.

Mr and Mrs Reuben can't have a baby, because Mrs Reuben is unable to carry a child. However, Mrs Artemis agrees that she will carry a child for them. Mr and Mrs Reuben provide the sperm and eggs, and fertilisation is carried out *in vitro*. Then two healthy embryos are implanted into Mrs Artemis' uterus. Nine months later, Mrs Artemis gives birth to a baby girl.

a) Who is the baby's:

   i) genetic mother? ....

   ii) surrogate mother? ....

b) Explain what is meant by *in vitro* fertilisation.

   ....

c) Two healthy embryos were implanted into Mrs Artemis' uterus.

   i) Suggest why two embryos were implanted.

   ....

   ii) Until quite recently, up to five embryos would usually be implanted in a single IVF treatment. Suggest why this is now not allowed.

   ....

Q2 The table shows the number of **IVF treatments** in a European country between 1990 and 2006.

YEAR	NO. OF TREATMENTS
1990	0
1992	2
1994	16
1996	55
1998	186
2000	348
2002	620
2004	740
2006	760

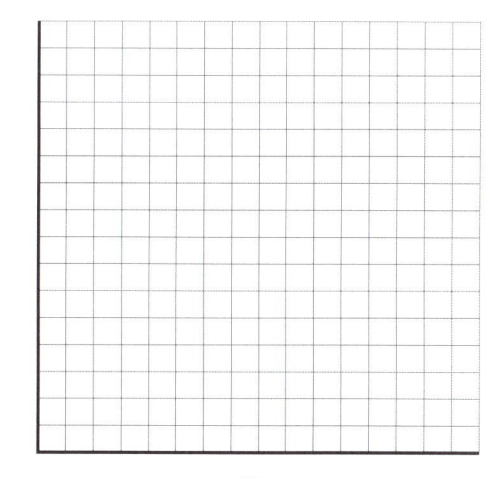

a) Plot this information on the grid provided.

b) Describe how the number of IVF treatments has changed during this time.

....

c) Suggest a possible reason for the trend that you have described.

....

B3 Topic 1 — Biotechnology

Reproductive Technology

Q3 Mr and Mrs Partridge have a child aged three, called Jason, who needs a **liver transplant**. They want to have a second child using **IVF**, and to choose an embryo with a **tissue match** for Jason, with the hope that the second child will be able to donate part of their liver.

    a) Explain why IVF (compared to normal fertilisation) makes it easier to have a child that will be a tissue match.

    ....

    ....

    b) The only reason for using the IVF procedure would be to find a tissue match for Jason.

        i) What would happen to embryos produced by the procedure that do not have matching tissues?

        ....

        ii) Explain why some people feel that this would not be justified.

        ....

        ....

        iii) Explain why other people feel that the procedure would be justified.

        ....

        ....

Q4 In the UK, it is legal to **screen** IVF embryos for **genetic disorders**, but it isn't usually legal to select the **sex** of the baby, and it isn't legal to screen them for other characteristics, such as eye colour.

    a) Give two reasons why it is considered undesirable for parents to choose characteristics of their baby, such as eye colour.

    ....

    ....

    b) In what circumstances are parents allowed to choose the sex of their baby?

    ....

    c) What is the advantage of screening for genetic disorders?

    ....

    d) Some people object to embryos being screened for genetic disorders. Suggest why.

    ....

Stem Cells

Q1 **Stem cell research** is a potentially exciting but very **controversial** area of biology.

a) Explain what a stem cell is.

....

b) Give one place where stem cells can be found in the body of an adult.

....

c) Explain what the following statement means: *"Every cell was once a stem cell"*.

....

....

d) If a stem cell divides to form other cells, what type of division is this?

....

Q2 The graph shows estimated **spending** on **stem cell research** in the UK between 1980 and 2005.

a) Describe how spending on this type of research has changed over the period shown.

....

b) Suggest explanations for:

   i) the low level of spending before 1990.

   ....

   ii) the change between 2001 and 2002.

   ....

c) Stem cell research may eventually lead to new treatments for several different diseases. Parkinson's disease is one example. Name two other diseases that could be treated using stem cells, and explain how the stem cells might be used in each case.

   1. ....

   2. ....

B3 Topic 1 — Biotechnology

Stem Cells

Q3 Some people are registered as **bone marrow donors**. Their bone marrow cells may be **transplanted** into a patient who needs them.

   a) Name one disease that bone marrow transplants might be used for.

   ....

   b) Bone marrow is a good source of **adult** stem cells, but stem cells from embryos are more useful from a medical point of view. Explain why.

   ....

   ....

Q4 Researchers were testing a new treatment. This involved injecting **embryonic stem cells** into the brains of patients with severe **Parkinson's disease**. After six months, the patients were tested to see if their symptoms had improved.

   a) What symptoms would the patients with severe Parkinson's disease have shown?

   ....

   b) If the treatment was successful, what would have happened to the stem cells inside the patients' brains?

   ....

   c) Suggest a suitable control experiment that could be used in this investigation.

   ....

   d) Give a possible ethical objection to this experiment, with regard to:

   i) the Parkinson's disease patients.

   ....

   ....

   ii) the source of the stem cells.

   ....

   ....

   e) How do researchers try to control what type of cells are produced from stem cells?

   ....

Top Tips: Some of the countries that **don't** allow embryonic stem cell research **do** still allow abortions and IVF treatment, which pro-research types argue is a rather strange lack of consistency.

B3 Topic 1 — Biotechnology

Mixed Questions — B3 Topic 1

Q1 Biochemists at the Gee-Fizz Drinks company use a **fungus** to synthesise **citric acid**.

a) Name a fungi that could be used in this process.

....

b) Explain why it's important to sterilise the container before the start of the process

....

....

c) What would you expect to happen to the pH of the container during fermentation? Explain your answer.

....

d) Gee-Fizz are currently developing low-calorie versions of their drinks.
Explain how they could use enzymes to produce a drink with fewer calories.

....

....

e) Eating a lot of foods high in sugar and fat can lead to obesity. Fats are required in the diet but in moderation. Give two functions of fats in the body.

1. .... 2. ....

f) Jamie is obese, he claims that it is not because of his lifestyle.
What else could have caused his obesity?

....

Q2 Mr and Mrs Milton have been trying to **conceive naturally** for the past three years but have so far been **unsuccessful**.

a) Give **three** reasons why they might not have been able to conceive naturally.

....

....

....

b) Treatments like IVF give couples like the Miltons the chance to be parents, however some people have ethical objections to IVF. Describe one ethical concern surrounding IVF.

....

....

B3 Topic 1 — Biotechnology

Mixed Questions — B3 Topic 1

Q3 A company have developed a maize crop that is **frost resistant**. This allows maize to be grown in areas that have previously been to cold for the crop.

  a) Describe how the frost-resistance gene is inserted into the maize.

  ....

  ....

  ....

  b) Some people are opposed to the genetic modification of plants. Discuss the reasons why.

  ....

  ....

  c) Modifying maize in this way is just one application of GM technology.
  Describe how the following modifications to plants might be an advantage for humans.

  i) Leaves that contain insecticide.

  ....

  ii) Crops with increased nutritional value.

  ....

Q4 Medi-gen is a company that is developing **new treatments** based on **genomics** (the study of organisms' genetic make-up).

  a) Describe three potential medical applications of genomics.

  ....

  ....

  ....

  ....

  b) Medi-gen have identified a potential drug in a substance found in a plant.
  Give two examples of drugs and the plants from which they have been obtained.

  ....

  ....

  c) The company is also planning a number of experiments involving stem cells.
  Explain how stem cells could be used to treat people with certain illnesses.

  ....

  ....

B3 Topic 1 — Biotechnology

Instinctive and Learned Behaviour

Q1 Read the following passage and fill in the missing words.

| genes | moisture | environment | learned | light | heat |

Most behaviours seen in animals are due to both inherited and .... factors.
Inherited aspects of behaviour depend on the animal's ....
An example of inherited behaviour is the negative phototaxis of earthworms, where they move away from ....

Q2 Match up the aspects of **human behaviour** to show whether they are **instinctive** or **learned**.

- Playing football
- Salivating
- Language
- Sneezing

- instinctive
- learned

Q3 A student was studying the behaviour of **birds** on a **bird table**. Each day the student provided small pieces of cheese, some nuts hanging from the table on lengths of string, and some corn.

Below are some of the observations made by the student:

1. Robins took the cheese, but ignored the nuts and corn.

2. Pigeons took corn, but ignored the cheese. They expressed interest in the hanging nuts, but weren't able to get at them.

3. Great tits took some of the cheese, and managed to hang from the strings to take the nuts.

Occasionally a single crow visited the bird table. It initially took the cheese and corn, and watched the great tits. After the third week the student recorded that the crow took the nuts, they were able to get at them by hanging from the string.

a) Give one example of a behaviour mentioned that seems to be **instinctive**, and explain your answer.

....

....

b) Give one example of a behaviour mentioned that is **learned**, giving a reason for your answer.

....

....

c) The student wanted to study how experiences in early life effect bird development. They kept a bird in isolation from a young age. What affect would you expect this to have on its song.

....

Top Tips: Animals are born with all the **nerve pathways** they need for **instinctive** behaviours **already connected**. The nerve pathways needed for **learned** behaviours develop with experience.

Instinctive and Learned Behaviour

Q4 An experiment was carried out into the **feeding behaviour** of **sea anemones**. Sea anemones are simple animals that live in marine rock pools, where they are found attached to rocks. Each has a ring of **tentacles** armed with stinging cells. Anemones use the stinging cells to paralyse smaller animals swimming in the water.

Two tanks of sea water each contained a single sea anemone. The behaviour of both the sea anemones was observed for **one hour**. A volume of 'fish extract' (made by crushing some dead fish in sea water) was placed in **one** of the tanks at a certain point within the hour of observation. The number of moving tentacles for each sea anemone was recorded at five minute intervals.

Time / minutes	No. of moving tentacles	
	Tank A	Tank B
0	2	2
5	1	1
10	10	2
15	7	0
20	4	2
30	3	0
40	4	0
50	4	1
60	4	2

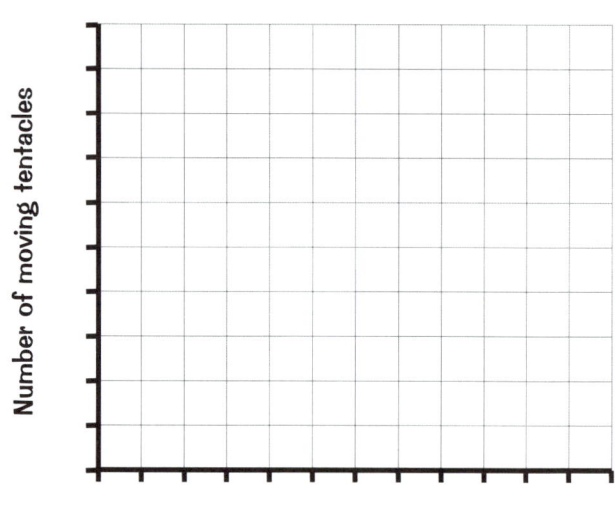

a) Draw graphs to illustrate the data on the grid provided. Use the same axes to show the results for both tanks.

b) Do you think the fish extract was added to tank A or to tank B? Explain your answer.

....

....

c) Suggest a time when the extract was added to the tank, giving a reason for your answer.

....

d) Suggest an explanation for what happened in the tank to which extract was added.

....

....

e) Do you think that this response is an example of learned or instinctive behaviour?

....

Q5 Explain what a **'Skinner box'** is and describe how it can be used to study animal behaviour.

....

....

....

B3 Topic 2 — Behaviour in Humans and Other Animals

Instinctive and Learned Behaviour

Q6 **Conditioning** is a type of **learned behaviour**.

a) Explain the difference between '**classical** conditioning' and '**operant** conditioning'.

....

....

....

....

b) Describe an example of:

i) classical conditioning ....

ii) operant conditioning ....

Q7 Identify each of the following examples of learned animal behaviour as either **classical conditioning** (C) or **operant conditioning** (O).

　　　　　　　　　　　　　　　　　　　　　　　　　　　　　　　　　　　　　C　O

a) A baby receives food, which makes it naturally happy. It only gets food when its mother is present. When its mother is present it feels happiness. ☐ ☐

b) A rat is provided with a maze, at the end of which is a food reward. After many trials, the rat learns to complete the maze and reach the reward without error. ☐ ☐

c) A child learns how to ride a bike. ☐ ☐

d) A dolphin learns to associate being given food with its trainer blowing a whistle. ☐ ☐

Q8 **Habituation** is an important part of the learning process in young animals.

a) Explain the term **habituation**.

....

....

b) Explain why habituation is **beneficial** to animals.

....

Q9 **Guide dogs** for the blind undergo a period of intensive **training**. One part of this training involves teaching the dogs to stop at roadsides and wait for commands.

a) Suggest one form of operant conditioning that could be used to ensure that the dog learns to stop at the roadside and wait for a command.

....

b) Explain why operant conditioning involving rewards is preferable to operant conditioning involving punishments.

....

B3 Topic 2 — Behaviour in Humans and Other Animals

Social Behaviour and Communication

Q1 List three reasons why animals **communicate** with one another.

1. ....

2. ....

3. ....

Q2 Below is a list of different **types** of communication used by different kinds of animals. In each case, suggest a **reason** for the communication.

a) A female moth releases a pheromone into the air.

....

b) A butterfly flashes its wings to show spots that look like large, staring eyes.

....

c) A honey bee does a 'waggle dance' in the hive.

....

d) A dog rolls onto its back. ....

Q3 **Peafowl** are large birds related to pheasants. Male peafowl, called **peacocks**, have long coloured feathers that project beyond the tail. Peafowl live naturally in India, where they are sometimes preyed on by tigers.

a) Suggest a possible **advantage** of the long feathers of the peacock.

....

b) Suggest a possible **disadvantage** of having these long feathers.

....

c) Female peafowl, called peahens, are dull-coloured in comparison. Suggest why.

....

....

Q4 **Language** is the most obvious form of **human communication**, but there are others.

a) Give three methods of **non-verbal** communication between humans.

....

b) What is a possible advantage of verbal communication over non-verbal communication?

....

B3 Topic 2 — Behaviour in Humans and Other Animals

Social Behaviour and Communication

Q5 The **chiffchaff** and the **willow warbler** are two related species of woodland birds. They are both green-brown in colour and spend much of their time among the foliage of trees.

a) Suggest why these birds attract mates using song rather than visual signals.

....

b) The song of the chiffchaff sounds very different from the song of a willow warbler. Explain why this is necessary.

....

....

Q6 **Communication** can happen in many different ways.

a) Humans communicate using **speech** and birds communicate using **song**. In what ways are these two forms of communication different?

....

....

b) Humans and many other mammals also use **facial expressions** to communicate. Would you expect a **panda bear** to understand a human **frown**? Explain your answer.

....

Q7 When confronted with a **mirror**, a **dog** may look behind the mirror in an attempt to find the 'other animal' presented to it. Suggest how this kind of reaction makes the behaviour of the dog fundamentally **different** from the behaviour of a typical human being.

....

....

Q8 It's thought that humans are more **self-aware** than other animals.

a) Explain what is meant by the term **self-awareness**.

....

....

....

b) Explain why it is difficult to know whether other animals have 'self-awareness'.

....

B3 Topic 2 — Behaviour in Humans and Other Animals

Feeding Behaviours

Q1 Choose words from the list below to complete the following passage.

| carnivores | vitamin A | herds | predators | amino acids | prey | herbivores | packs |

Sheep, cows, horses and rabbits are ...., which means that they feed on plant material. Many feed in groups called .... This makes it more likely that at least a few individuals will be able to spot .... A problem with a herbivorous diet is that it can be low in certain kinds of nutrients, such as ...., so herbivores have to spend a lot of time feeding.

Q2 The diagrams to the right show a **sheep skull** and a **cat skull**. Sheep are herbivores and cats are carnivores.

a) A sheep's eyes are on the **side** of its head, but a cat's eyes are at the **front**. Suggest why each species has evolved these features.

....

....

b) Give one other difference between the skulls that could be related to different types of feeding.

....

....

Q3 **Wolves** work in packs when hunting large animals such as **reindeer**.

a) Suggest why it is important for wolves to cooperate in this way when they hunt reindeer.

....

b) Reindeer are usually found in **herds**. Give two reasons why this reduces the chances of any one particular reindeer being caught by a wolf pack.

....

....

....

c) Explain why large herds of herbivores need to move around frequently.

....

d) Wolves usually hunt **individually** for smaller prey such as rabbits. Suggest why.

....

B3 Topic 2 — Behaviour in Humans and Other Animals

Feeding Behaviours

Q4 Which of the following statements are most likely to apply to **herbivores**, and which to **carnivores**?

		herbivores	carnivores
a)	They have strong horns for defence.	☐	☐
b)	They eat food that is high in protein.	☐	☐
c)	They can go for several days without feeding.	☐	☐
d)	They form groups with others of the same species for safety.	☐	☐
e)	They form groups with others of the same species to get food.	☐	☐

Q5 Read the following passage about the feeding behaviour of **spiders**.

> All spiders are predators. They have fangs connected to poison glands. When they bite prey with their fangs, they inject the poison which quickly paralyses the prey. Some spiders ambush their prey, either by leaping on them (in the case of jumping spiders), or running them down (as with wolf spiders). Many spiders have glands that produce silk, which they use to spin webs — the webs produced by money spiders and orb-web spiders are used to trap flying insects. Funnel-web spiders lay trip-lines for their prey, and lie in wait for them in holes in the ground.

a) Give two **structural** features of spiders that make them good predators.

....

b) The poison of many spiders works so quickly that the prey is paralysed almost immediately. Suggest why it is important that the poison works quickly.

....

c) Describe three ways in which different spiders catch their prey.

....

....

Q6 Some animals use **tools** to get food.

a) Give two examples of animals using tools.

1. ....

2. ....

b) Some species of vulture break open bones to reach the nutritious marrow inside by dropping the bones onto rocks. Would you class the rocks as tools in this case? Explain your answer.

....

....

B3 Topic 2 — Behaviour in Humans and Other Animals

Feeding Behaviours

Q7 Adult **birds** respond to **stimuli** from their young, which prompt them to supply **food**.

a) Describe the ways in which parent birds may be stimulated to feed their offspring.

....

....

b) Explain why both parent and young are using instinctive (inherited) behaviour when a bird feeds its offspring.

....

....

Q8 Experiments were carried out to investigate the **'begging response'** in young **herring gulls**. The young peck at the bill of the parent to stimulate it to regurgitate fish, which the young then swallow. This behaviour occurs soon after the young hatch. Scientists presented young herring gulls with a series of **cardboard models** of a parent gull's head. The results of the study are shown below. Real adult herring gulls have a **white head**, with a **yellow bill** and a **red spot** near the tip.

Model	White head, grey bill, no spot	White head, grey bill, red spot	White head, yellow bill, red spot	Pointed red stick with three white bands
No. of pecks by young	5	39	42	50

a) Describe what these experiments demonstrate about what stimulates the begging response in young herring gulls. Explain your answer.

....

....

....

b) Is the begging response instinctive or learned? Give a reason for your answer.

....

....

c) It's thought that parent birds are also stimulated to regurgitate food by the wide open, brightly coloured mouths of chicks begging for food. Describe how you could test whether it's the **colour** or the **size** of a chick's open mouth (or both) which stimulates the parent to regurgitate food.

....

....

B3 Topic 2 — Behaviour in Humans and Other Animals

Reproductive Behaviours

Q1 Draw lines to match up each animal below with the most likely way in which a **male** of that species would **attract a mate**.

mandrill monkey

red deer

frog

moth

display aggression to other males

mating call

pheromone

display brightly coloured parts of body

Q2 Explain what is meant by the following terms:

a) monogamy

....

b) harem

....

c) courtship

....

Q3 In many species of **birds**, **both** parents play a role in incubating eggs and feeding the young once the eggs have hatched.

a) State an advantage of this shared responsibility for:

i) the young. ....

....

ii) the parents. ....

....

b) **Birds of paradise** differ in that the females have sole responsibility for looking after the young. These birds live on the island of New Guinea, where there are few predators.

Suggest a possible link between the reproductive behaviour of birds of paradise and the fact that there are few predators in their habitat.

....

....

....

B3 Topic 2 — Behaviour in Humans and Other Animals

Reproductive Behaviours

Q4 In most species, **males compete** to win the right to mate with females. Methods used vary from bringing the female gifts of food to fighting off the other males. However, it is the **opposite** way around in **seahorses** — females compete for the attention of males. Seahorses are also unusual in that the female lays her eggs in the male's pouch and **he** is then '**pregnant**' with the young and eventually gives birth to them.

a) Explain fully why males usually compete for females, and why this is not the case in seahorses.

....
....
....
....
....

b) Why is it important for most animals that females don't mate with a male of a closely related species?

....
....

Q5 Some young birds and mammals develop a simple kind of behaviour early in their life called '**imprinting**', where learned behaviour becomes fixed and resistant to change. Ducklings, for example, develop imprinted behaviour when they **instinctively follow** the first thing they see move — which usually is their mother.

a) The imprinting behaviour of ducklings is inherited and not learned. Explain how you can tell this from the description above.

....
....

b) Give one advantage of imprinting behaviour in ducklings.

....
....

c) Suggest one part of a duckling's behaviour that will be learned, rather than inherited.

....

Top Tips: The male **bowerbird** impresses females by constructing an elaborate mound of earth decorated lavishly with shells, leaves, feathers and flowers, which he spends **hours** carefully arranging.

B3 Topic 2 — Behaviour in Humans and Other Animals

Reproductive Behaviours

Q6 Some animals **care for their young** for long periods, while others provide **no parental care** at all.

a) Name three animals that care for their young, and three that do not.

Care: ....

Don't care: ....

b) Give three ways in which animals may care for their young.

1. ....

2. ....

3. ....

Q7 Male **crickets** and **grasshoppers** attract females by a process called '**stridulation**', where they rub rough parts of their body together. Crickets rubs their wings together and grasshoppers rub their legs over their wings. The result is a **chirping sound**.

a) Different species of crickets and grasshoppers produce different patterns of chirps, in terms of volume, pitch and frequency of chirps. Explain why.

....

....

b) The 'songs' of different species of grasshopper are more distinctive than the songs of different species of cricket. What does this suggest about the **appearance** of different species of the two kinds of insects. Explain your answer.

....

....

....

Q8 Parental care is a **successful evolutionary strategy**.

a) Explain why.

....

....

b) Why is a shorter pregnancy less risky to a mother than a long pregnancy?

....

....

B3 Topic 2 — Behaviour in Humans and Other Animals

Reproductive Behaviours

Q9 In some mammals the young are born very **well developed**. Horses, for example, give birth to young that can quickly stand and walk. Other mammals, such as kangaroos, give birth to young at a very **early stage** in their development — these are blind and helpless. Suggest an **advantage** and a **disadvantage** of **each method** of producing young.

Horses. ....

....

....

Kangaroos. ....

....

....

Q10 The table compares the **average number of offspring** produced per female per year for some different animal species.

Species	Average no. of offspring per year
Oran-utan	0.25
Wood mouse	20
Sperm whale	0.1
Red fox	5
Green turtle	200

a) Explain how it is possible for the average number of offspring per year of the orang-utan and the sperm whale to be less than one.

....

....

b) On average, a female wood mouse gives birth to **five** offspring after a pregnancy. Explain how 20 offspring can be produced per year.

....

c) Which species of animal is likely to show the least degree of parental care? Give a full explanation for your answer.

....

....

....

....

B3 Topic 2 — Behaviour in Humans and Other Animals

Human Evolution and Development

Q1 Scientists think that humans are most **closely related** to a species of ape called a **bonobo**.

a) Explain how scientists know this.

....

b) Give one difference in behaviour between humans and bonobos.

....

Q2 Suggest how each of the following has contributed to the **success** of the **human species**:

a) Tool use.

....

....

b) Living in large, complex societies.

....

....

Q3 Below are some of the key events in the **evolution** of **human behaviour**.

> **2.5 million yrs ago** — earliest use of stone tools.
>
> **50 000 yrs ago** — hunter-gatherer society.
>
> **10 000 years ago** — farming begins in some parts of the world.

a) Explain what is meant by 'hunter-gatherer society'.

....

....

b) Explain how the use of tools would have been beneficial in such a society.

....

....

c) Suggest one advantage of a farming system over a hunter-gatherer system.

....

....

B3 Topic 2 — Behaviour in Humans and Other Animals

Human Evolution and Development

Q4 Humans have **domesticated** a range of animal species.

a) Dogs were one of the first species to become domesticated.
Explain the advantage to the humans living at this time of domesticating dogs.

....

....

b) Choose reasons from the list below for domesticating the following animals.

| **A** For hide | **B** Farming the land | **C** For Food |
| **D** For travelling | **E** Carrying heavy loads | **F** For a table tennis partner |

Horse: ....

Cattle: ....

c) Give one example of how selective breeding has been used to modify the characteristics of a domesticated animal.

....

....

Q5 'Human' society has changed significantly in the last two million years.

a) Give three main ways in which we currently modify our environment.

1. ....

2. ....

3. ....

b) We use **tools** to modify our environment. Other animals, e.g. chimps, also use tools.
Suggest why humans rather than chimps have been able to develop farming and build cities.

....

....

Top Tips: Our ancestors used to swing through trees. Then they started to walk on two legs a bit. They gradually left the trees and, about two million years ago, began to use simple **tools** — and then it was just a short hop, skip and jump to playstations and microwaves.

B3 Topic 2 — Behaviour in Humans and Other Animals

Human Behaviour Towards Animals

Q1 Name **one animal** that is used for each purpose given below.

  a) Providing wool ....

  b) Hunted for sport ....

  c) Racing ....

Q2 Many different species of animal are kept in **zoos**. Some people think that this is **necessary**, but others think it is **cruel**. Outline the reasons for and against keeping animals in zoos.

....

....

....

....

Q3 Animals are often used to test **drugs** before they are released for human use.

  a) Explain why many people think this is necessary.

  ....

  b) Suggest one reason why some people feel it is cruel to use animals in this way.

  ....

  They're looking for a bit more in these than 'because it's cruel'.

  c) Give one other way in which laboratory animals could be of use in medicine.

  ....

Q4 Some people feel that animals should have the **same rights** as humans.

  a) Animals are used for entertainment in some circuses.

   i) Give one reason why some people might be against this.

   ....

   ii) Explain how a circus owner might justify this use of the animals.

   ....

  b) Animals are also bred for food. They are often intensively farmed. Explain:

   i) why some people think that this is wrong.

   ....

   ii) how this use of animals could be justified.

   ....

B3 Topic 2 — Behaviour in Humans and Other Animals

Mixed Questions — B3 Topic 2

Q1 Many people keep **dogs** either as **companions** or as **working** animals. The domesticated dog is similar in many ways to **wild dogs** which live in parts of Africa.

   a) A domesticated dog can be taught to 'sit' by rewarding it every time it responds correctly to the 'sit' command. What type of conditioning is this an example of? Underline the correct answer.

   classical   operant

   b) Many domesticated dogs are useful as guards, because they will bark loudly if they hear a burglar breaking into the house, but don't bark at noises from people or cars just passing the house.

   i) Explain why dogs respond to the quiet noise of a burglar but not to the louder noise from cars.

   ....

   ....

   ii) Give two other examples of how dogs are useful to humans, apart from guarding property and providing companionship.

   ....

   c) Both wild dogs and domesticated dogs feed their young on milk for several weeks after birth. How does a newborn puppy 'know' to suckle from its mother?

   ....

   d) African wild dogs are carnivores. Their prey includes gazelles (shown in the picture), which are herbivores. Gazelles spend much more time **eating** than wild dogs do. Explain this difference.

   ....

   ....

   e) After birth, young wild dogs spend several months with their parents, who protect them from predators and teach them to hunt effectively.

   i) Outline the possible **disadvantages** for the parents of this behaviour.

   ....

   ii) Explain why this behaviour is a **good evolutionary strategy**, despite its disadvantages.

   ....

   ....

Q2 **Swans** mate for life — once a pair have mated, they only breed with each other. Explain why this behaviour is unusual, and describe some more common mating patterns.

....

....

B3 Topic 2 — Behaviour in Humans and Other Animals

Mixed Questions — B3 Topic 2

Q3 **Wildebeest** are a type of buffalo which graze on **short grass**. During the dry season they move from place to place in large **herds**. Wildebeest are commonly preyed on by **lions**.

a) Why do you think herds of wildebeest have to move frequently during the dry season?

....

b) Explain why it is advantageous for the wildebeest to move and graze in large herds.

....

....

Q4 **Humans** are closely related to **bonobos** (a kind of ape) and share many **behaviours** with them.

a) It's thought that humans first developed agriculture about 10 000 years ago. Before then, how did humans obtain food?

....

b) In every part of the world, humans **smile** as a way of communicating **pleasure**. Would you expect bonobos to show pleasure by smiling? Explain your answer.

....

c) Both humans and apes (like bonobos) can use tools, and communicate in a variety of ways. Describe three ways in which humans are thought to be very **different** from all other animals.

....

....

....

....

Q5 Most **birds** reproduce by laying a **small** clutch of eggs, and keeping them warm until they hatch into **chicks**. They then tend the chicks in the nest for several weeks.

a) **Frogs** lay **large** clumps of frogspawn in a pond and then leave — they don't tend the spawn or the tadpoles which hatch from it. Explain why frogs don't need to look after their young but birds do.

....

....

b) The 'cheeping' of a young bird stimulates its parent to feed it. Give three other 'uses' of bird calls.

....

....

B3 Topic 2 — Behaviour in Humans and Other Animals

Mixed Questions — B3 Topic 2

Q6 **Male frigate birds** have red sacs on their chests. During the mating season, males **display** by inflating this sac, as shown in the picture.

a) What advantage might the male frigate bird gain from this behaviour?

....

b) In most bird species the female is **duller** in appearance than the male. Explain why this is.

....

....

Q7 **Golden eagles** are large birds of prey. Their diet includes smaller birds like **grouse** and mammals like **rabbits**. They catch their prey by diving down quickly and plucking it from the ground.

a) Golden eagles hunt as individuals.

   i) Some carnivores hunt in packs. What advantages can this give them?

   ....

   ii) Suggest why golden eagles **don't** hunt in packs.

   ....

b) Golden eagles have eyes at the **front** of their heads. Explain how this is important in terms of their feeding behaviour.

....

....

c) Suggest features of the following animals which help them avoid being caught by a golden eagle:

   i) rabbits ....

   ....

   ....

   ii) grouse ....

   ....

   ....

B3 Topic 2 — Behaviour in Humans and Other Animals